A Complete Guide to Docker for Operations and Development

Test-Prep for the Docker Certified Associate (DCA) Exam

Engy Fouda

Apress®

A Complete Guide to Docker for Operations and Development: Test-Prep for the Docker Certified Associate (DCA) Exam

Engy Fouda
Hopewell Junction, NY, USA

ISBN-13 (pbk): 978-1-4842-8116-1   ISBN-13 (electronic): 978-1-4842-8117-8
https://doi.org/10.1007/978-1-4842-8117-8

Managing Director, Apress Media LLC: Welmoed Spahr
Acquisitions Editor: Aditee Mirashi
Development Editor: James Markham
Coordinating Editor: Aditee Mirashi

Cover designed by eStudioCalamar

Cover image designed by Freepik (www.freepik.com)

Distributed to the book trade worldwide by Springer Science+Business Media New York, 1 New York Plaza, Suite 4600, New York, NY 10004-1562, USA. Phone 1-800-SPRINGER, fax (201) 348-4505, e-mail orders-ny@springer-sbm.com, or visit www.springeronline.com. Apress Media, LLC is a California LLC and the sole member (owner) is Springer Science + Business Media Finance Inc (SSBM Finance Inc). SSBM Finance Inc is a **Delaware** corporation.

For information on translations, please e-mail booktranslations@springernature.com; for reprint, paperback, or audio rights, please e-mail bookpermissions@springernature.com.

Apress titles may be purchased in bulk for academic, corporate, or promotional use. eBook versions and licenses are also available for most titles. For more information, reference our Print and eBook Bulk Sales web page at http://www.apress.com/bulk-sales.

Any source code or other supplementary material referenced by the author in this book is available to readers on GitHub via the book's product page, located at www.apress.com/978-1-4842-8116-1. For more detailed information, please visit http://www.apress.com/source-code.

Printed on acid-free paper

*To my motivator and daughter, Areej, who talks about me
with proudness and makes me extremely happy.
To my husband, Hesham, who does everything he can do to support
me. To my hero and dad, Dr. Mohamed Samir, you are my role model.
Every single day, I try to be you. To my mom, Dr. Suzan, who knows
how to celebrate my achievements. To my brother, aunts, nieces,
nephews, and cousins, I wish I could celebrate this new book with you.*

Table of Contents

About the Author

Engy Fouda is an adjunct lecturer at SUNY New Paltz teaching Intro to Data Science using SAS Studio and Introduction to Machine Learning using Python. She is an Apress and Packt Publishing author. Currently, she teaches SAS, Docker, and Kubernetes tracks at ONLC (Microsoft Partner) and other venues as a freelance instructor. She also works as a freelance editor at the Polaris&Dawn company. She holds two master's degrees: one in journalism from Harvard University, the Extension School and the other in computer engineering from Cairo University. Moreover, she earned a Data Science Graduate Professional Certificate from Harvard University, the Extension School. She volunteers as the executive manager and is a former team leader for Momken Group (Engineering for the Blind), Egypt Scholars Inc.

About the Technical Reviewer

 **Onur Yilmaz** is a senior software engineer at a multinational enterprise software company. He is a Certified Kubernetes Administrator (CKA) and works on Kubernetes and cloud management systems as a keen supporter of cutting-edge technologies. Furthermore, he is the author of multiple books on Kubernetes, Docker, serverless architectures, and cloud-native continuous integration and delivery. In addition, he has one master's and two bachelor's degrees in the engineering field.

PART I

Docker Fundamentals

CHAPTER 1

Introduction

The book's scope is to help you pass the Docker Certified Associate (DCA) exam. Earning the certificate is proof of your experience in working with containers; the Mirantis Kubernetes Engine (MKE), formerly known as the Docker Enterprise Engine; swarms; clusters; and containerized applications.

Getting certified sets your minimum salary and helps you present yourself in the market. Moreover, plenty of corporations set being certified as a condition to get hired.

This prep book will cover all the topics that you will be tested on during the exam and more. You will learn how to install and use the Universal Control Plane (UCP) and the Docker Trusted Registry (DTR). Moreover, it has plenty of real exam questions from previous exams to practice. This book will help you identify your strengths and weaknesses and guide you on how to increase your knowledge in the weak topics.

Who Should Read This Book?

The book's primary targets are system administrators, operations managers, developers, and IT professionals who would seek to pass the DCA exam. The book assumes that you have some experience with Docker and Kubernetes and are looking to get certified.

However, the book is helpful for anyone looking for these topics in-depth and learning them. It provides detailed explanations of the concepts with hands-on examples in a step-by-step format.

How This Book Is Organized

The book is divided into two parts and follows the main outline of the exam sections. However, it covers even more than that. In Part 1, Chapters 1–12, you will find some extra chapters covering topics you will need in your practical workdays on which you will not be tested. Those chapters providing extra information will not have quizzes for them.

© Engy Fouda 2022
E. Fouda, *A Complete Guide to Docker for Operations and Development*,
https://doi.org/10.1007/978-1-4842-8117-8_1

In Part 2, Chapters 13–18, you will find quizzes for the chapters that are included in the exam only.

Chapters 2–5, 10, and 11 all cover exam sections. Chapters 6–9 are not explicitly in the exam, but you cannot work without knowing this information. Chapter 12 tries to focus on the exam steps and how to register. Chapters 13–18 have a sample of real exam questions.

Exam Topics

The exam covers the following topics:

- Orchestration (25% of the exam)

- Image creation, management, and registry (20% of the exam)

- Installation and configuration (15% of the exam)

- Networking (15% of the exam)

- Security (15% of the exam)

- Storage and volumes (10% of the exam)

You must pass every section of the exam and get more than 50% in the total. If you failed any section, you would fail the whole test.

What You Will Learn

- Learn the difference between the container and the virtual machine, the lifecycle of the container, and the various stages of development.

- Know how to install Docker on various platforms and how to manage the resources.

- Create your first container and image. Push and pull to and from the registry hub. Learn how to install your own local registry.

- Mount volumes.

- Learn all about container networking.

- Orchestrate between containers and learn how to debug your containers.

- Learn how to create a swarm and prepare your containers for production.

- Write a Dockerfile, Docker Compose YAML file, and Kubernetes manifest YAML file.

- Learn how to install the Docker Enterprise Edition (EE)/Mirantis Kubernetes Engine (MKE) with client shell.

- Learn how Docker achieves agility, portability, and control for developers and the IT operations team across all stages of the app lifecycle.

- Learn all about the exam and how to pass it, and work on plenty of real exam questions from previous exams to practice.

Summary

This chapter provided an overview of the road map to getting certified. It listed how the book is organized, the target audience, and the exam sections and their coverage percentages.

CHAPTER 2

Installation and Configuration

There are two Docker editions: Community Edition (CE, entirely free) and Enterprise Edition (EE, not free). This chapter will focus on Docker Community Edition (CE) installation. Chapters 6, 7, and 8 will show in detail how to install, configure, and use the Docker Enterprise Edition and its components. This chapter lists the common configuration commands between the two editions. Many of the exam questions test you on these common commands.

It is crucial to mention that the installation and configuration exam section is covered in this chapter and the chapters mentioned earlier. Moreover, this chapter's sections are not interconnected, but all lie under the installation and configuration exam section.

The chapter will cover the following topics:

1. How to install the Docker CE for various operating systems

2. The difference between containerization and virtualization

3. How to set up a local registry

4. Configuration of logging drivers

5. How to set up a swarm, configure managers, add nodes, and scale your system

6. The usage of namespaces and cgroups

© Engy Fouda 2022
E. Fouda, *A Complete Guide to Docker for Operations and Development*,
https://doi.org/10.1007/978-1-4842-8117-8_2

How to Install the Docker CE for Various Operating Systems

Docker has editions that can be installed on various operating systems. They are available on Docker Hub: https://hub.docker.com/search?type=edition&offering=community.

For Ubuntu, use this command: wget -qO- https://get.docker.com/ | sh.

For Microsoft Windows, enable Hyper-V and enable virtualization. If virtualization is not enabled, enter the computer BIOS, and enable it. For Windows 10 Professional or Enterprise 64-bit or Windows 10 Home 64-bit with WSL 2, install Docker Desktop for Windows. It is a pretty straightforward step: download the exe file and follow the instructions.

However, for Windows 7, 8, and 10 Home, use Docker Toolbox, and use Oracle VirtualBox. Every time, you'll need to click the Kitematic (Alpha) icon, as in Figure 2-1.

Figure 2-1. *Kitematic (Alpha) icon*

After Kitematic starts successfully, double-click the Docker Quickstart Terminal icon, as in Figure 2-2.

Figure 2-2. *Docker Quickstart Terminal*

If the host's operating system is Windows and Ubuntu is installed inside a virtual machine on top of it, avoid the "VboxClient Fail To Start" error on Ubuntu VirtualBox guest machines by following this link:

`https://websiteforstudents.com/how-to-fix-vboxclient-fail-to-start-error-on-ubuntu-virtalbox-guest-machines/`

There are no questions in the DCA exam about this point, but it can cause issues in the installation, causing you to not be able to do the rest of the book's hands-on labs.

Difference Between Containerization and Virtualization

Virtual machines represent hardware-level virtualization where one operating system is downloaded on top of a host operating system. Therefore, they are heavy and fully isolated. There is no availability for SSH or TTY, and they are fully secured.

On the other hand, containers represent operating system virtualization. You can download as many different operating systems in containers as applications need. Containers are light and fast; however, they are not fully isolated but secure, as discussed in Chapter 11.

How to Set Up a Local Registry

A Docker registry is a location where Docker images can be pushed, pulled, and stored. Registered users have their own spaces in the registry. This user-named space is called repository. A repository is a namespace that is used for storing images. For example, assume a user has a public image called `firstapp` that is pushed to Docker Hub. To reach to this image, one must use the image repository name, which is `<username>/<image name>`. In this example, assume that I am the image owner. Then the image repository is `engyfouda/firstapp`.

Registries can be hosted by a third party as a public or private registry. Docker Hub is an example of it. Later in the book, we will learn about the Docker Trusted Registry and how to install it and use it with the Docker EE. Also, there are Google Container Registry and AWS Container Registry.

Let us see how to set up and use a local registry. Setting it up is easy and fast. It is only one command as we will see. To test it, we will pull any image from Docker Hub, then push it to our local registry, delete all the local images, and pull it from the local registry.

To set up a local registry without a graphical user interface (GUI), we will use a repository image that is on Docker Hub called Registry with tag 2 (registry:2). The installation command is `docker run -d -p 5000:5000 --restart=always --name registry registry:2`. Basically, we craft a container based on the `registry:2` image. The `-d` option is to run as a daemon in the background. The `-p` is to set the <host port>: <container port>; we will talk about ports in detail in Chapter 4. We set the `restart` policy to be `always` and set the container name as `registry`.

To test this registry, we pull any image from Docker Hub, for example, `docker pull busybox`. Then rename it to add the local repository name using `docker tag busybox localhost:5000/firstapp`. Now, push it to the local registry using `docker push localhost:5000/firstapp`. Delete all the local images using `docker image remove busybox` and `docker image remove localhost:5000/firstapp`. To make sure that we do not have trace of these images, list the images using `docker image ls`, and we will not find these images in the list anymore. Pull the image from our local registry: `docker pull localhost:5000/firstapp`.

To remove the local registry, stop it and remove it using `docker container stop registry && docker container rm -v registry`.

To add a GUI, follow the steps in this site: `http://joxit.github.io/docker-registry-ui/`.

Configuration of Logging Drivers

By default, Docker uses the json-file logging driver, which caches container logs as JSON internally. To catch the log, use the `docker logs <Container ID or name>` subcommand.

There are other drivers that Docker can use, for example, splunk, journald, and none to disable logging. To configure the logging driver, run the `docker run -it --log-driver <log driver> <image>` subcommand.

To fetch the driver type, run `docker inspect -f '{{.HostConfig.LogConfig.Type}}' <CONTAINER>`.

The Usage of Namespaces and Cgroups

Every container is isolated from other containers and has its own resources. These resources are called namespaces, for example, the PID (Process ID), PPID (Parent Process ID), network, mount, and others. The full isolation between containers ensures security and prohibits one container from going inside another one and messing it up.

Another basic security feature in Docker is cgroups, which represent the shared resources between containers, for example, the CPU, memory, and disk I/O. Docker has sensible defaults for not allowing one container to overtake the shared resources and not allowing any other container to use them.

How to Set Up a Swarm, Configure Managers, Add Nodes, and Scale Your System

This section presents a basic introduction to production with a Docker swarm. We will learn it in detail later in the book. At first, we will learn how to build the simplest swarm of one manager and one worker. Then later in the hands-on lab, we will learn how to scale up the number of nodes and how to configure it and specify which nodes are managers and which are workers.

First, Build a Simple Swarm of One Manager and One Worker

1. Go to `https://labs.play-with-docker.com`. In Chapters 6, 7, and 8, we will learn how to create several nodes on the same machine using docker-machine. In the real world, each node can be a server, a Raspberry Pi, a single computer, or a handheld.

2. Add two new instances: node 1 is a manager, and node 2 is a worker.

3. Note: The usual key shortcuts for copying and pasting will not work. To copy, use Ctrl+Insert and to paste, use Shift+Insert.

4. To initialize a swarm, run `docker swarm init --advertise-addr <IP>`. The IP is at the top of the Docker playground page. A

token command will be generated to add more nodes. Copy this command.

5. Paste the command and run it on node 2 to add it as a worker to the cluster.

6. Return to the first node. To list all the nodes that we have in our cluster, run `docker node ls`.

7. Create a new overlay network using `docker network create -d overlay mynet`. In Chapter 4, we will learn more about network types.

8. To run a service, run `docker service create --name myservice --network mynet --publish published=80, target=80,mode=host --replicas 2 engyfouda/ kgpoundconverter:linux`.

9. To list the services, run `docker service ls`.

10. Run `docker service ps myservice`.

Second, Let Us Scale Up to Five Replicas

1. Assume that the business is booming and we need more nodes to meet our clients' requests. For this example, we will scale to five nodes only because Docker playground allows only five instances.

2. Always better to use an odd number of managers. We will talk about the best practices in Chapter 4.

3. Hence, our new cluster will be three managers and two workers.

4. Create three more instances – nodes 3, 4, 5 – by clicking the `Create new instance` button.

5. On node 1, run the `docker swarm join-token` manager to get the token for adding managers. Run this instruction on nodes 3 and 4.

6. Similarly, to get the token to add a worker, run `docker swarm join-token worker`.

7. Run the token instruction on node number 5.

8. To list all the nodes, run `docker node ls`.

9. It will show the five nodes, having node 1 as leader and nodes 3 and 4 as managers.

10. On node 1, run `docker service scale myservice=5` to scale the service to have five replicas of the service.

11. To see which replica is running on which node, run `docker service ps myservice`.

12. On node 1, run `docker service rm myservice` to remove the service.

13. To remove the network, run `docker network rm mynet`.

Summary

The installation and configuration exam section is covered in several chapters in this book. This chapter is the first one, covering the installation of the Docker CE only. Also, it covered the difference between containerization and virtualization, how to set up a local registry, and the configuration of logging drivers. Moreover, it covered how to set up a swarm, configure managers, add nodes, and scale your system and the usage of namespaces and cgroups.

CHAPTER 3

Image Creation, Management, and Registry

In this chapter, you will learn how to create images and containers through an easy flow. The tricky questions in the exam usually focus on the multistage builds, the Dockerfile commands, the health check in the Dockerfile, the inspect command options, and the client commands to manage images.

Therefore, the chapter will cover the following topics:

- The flow including the CLI commands to manage images and containers

- The Dockerfile commands in the flow

- The inspect command

- The multistage build and how to optimize your images

Docker Flow

The Docker flow starts with a command on the client (CLI) pulling an image using the `docker pull` subcommand, as in Figure 3-1. The Docker engine checks if the image is locally at the host or not. If it is not, the engine will pull it from the repository. Then it runs it and crafts a container from that image using the `docker run` subcommand. Think of an image as a stack of layers. The container is the last layer at the top, where you can manipulate it and add whatever commands and packages on top of the base image. You can save this new image that includes the old parent one and all the new addition using

© Engy Fouda 2022
E. Fouda, *A Complete Guide to Docker for Operations and Development*,
https://doi.org/10.1007/978-1-4842-8117-8_3

the docker commit subcommand or using the Dockerfile. The final step in the flow is to push the image to the repository, and you do that using the docker push subcommand.

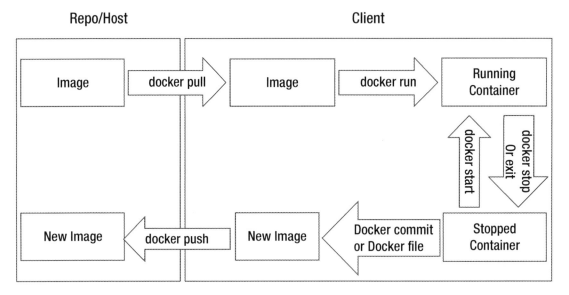

Figure 3-1. *The Docker flow*

In Docker, there are two sets of commands: the old and the new. The old or the legacy set is only two levels. The first level is docker, and the second one is the subcommand, as docker pull <image name>. The new and standard one is three levels. The first level is docker, the second is the object, and the third is the subcommand. Images, containers, networks, nodes, and volumes are examples of Docker objects. In this case, the command to pull an image is docker image pull <image name>. The exam uses the new, three-level commands. Therefore, in the book, we will use the new standard set of commands.

Pulling an Image

Let us now follow the flow step-by-step, as in Figure 3-2. We shall start with pulling the image.

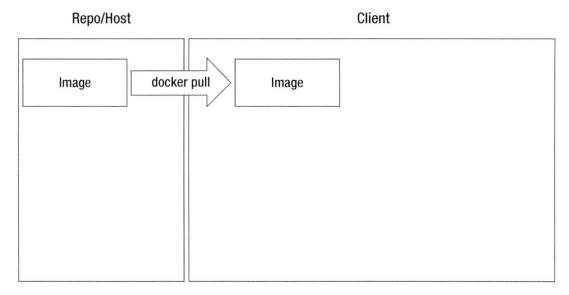

Figure 3-2. *Pulling the image*

At the shell prompt, as in Listing 3-1, type `docker image pull alpine`. The Docker engine will pull the alpine image for you. To verify that it has been pulled correctly, list the images stored on your Docker host using `docker image ls`. Congratulations! You just downloaded your first image!

Listing 3-1. Pulling an image and listing all the images at the host

```
$ docker image pull alpine
Using default tag: latest
latest: Pulling from library/alpine
5843afab3874: Pulling fs layer
5843afab3874: Verifying Checksum
5843afab3874: Pull complete
Digest: sha256:234cb88d3020898631af0ccbbcca9a66ae7306ecd30c972069085
8c1b007d2a0
Status: Downloaded newer image for alpine:latest
docker.io/library/alpine:latest

$ docker image ls
REPOSITORY      TAG         IMAGE ID        CREATED         SIZE
alpine          latest      d4ff818577bc    3 weeks ago     5.6MB
```

The output of `docker image ls` shows the following:

- REPOSITORY: This is the name of the image. In this example, the repository name is alpine.

- TAG: This is the image tag or version. Any image can have several tags for the same image ID. The Docker engine assigns `latest` as the default tag.

- IMAGE ID: Every image can have several tags but will have one unique 64-hex digit ID. The Docker engine autogenerates it. In the default display, Docker will show the first 12 digits only. To display all the 64 digits, type this at the shell: `docker image ls --no-trunc`.

- CREATED: Shows when the image was created.

- SIZE: Shows the size of the image.

Note   If you use Ubuntu and receive the following error

`Error response from daemon: Get https://registry-1. docker.io/v2/: dial tcp: lookup registry-1.docker.io on 192.168.65.1:53: serv`

type sudo nano /etc/resolv.conf.

Change nameserver to 8.8.8.8.

Save and then retry downloading the image.

Crafting a Container

Now, you will create your first container based on the alpine image that you downloaded, as in Figure 3-3. Type this at the shell: `docker container run alpine echo "hello my first container"`.

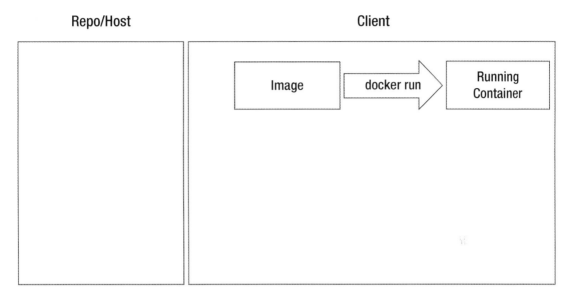

Figure 3-3. *Run your first container*

The Docker engine will echo the sentence for you, as in Listing 3-2. To list all the containers you have, run `docker container ls -a`. In this command, the `ls` is for listing all the running containers. The `-a` option is to list all the containers, whatever their statuses are. Hurray! You ran your first container!

Listing 3-2. Running a container

```
$ docker container run alpine echo "hello my first container"
ww$ docker container ls -a
CONTAINER ID   IMAGE    COMMAND                      CREATED
STATUS       PORTS             NAMES
d99b153cf127  alpine   "echo 'hello my firs..."  22 minutes ago
Exited (0) 22 minutes ago   xenodochial_stonebraker
```

The output shows the following:

- CONTAINER ID: The unique ID that the engine autogenerated. Again, similar to the image ID, it is 64 hex digits. By default, the first 12 only will be shown for readability. All the objects in Docker will follow this similar paradigm.

- IMAGE: Shows the base page from where this container was crafted.

- COMMAND: The initial command that you sent while running the container.

- CREATED: The timestamp of creating the container.

- STATUS: Shows the current status of the container. It can be running or exited as in this example, created, running (paused). You can change the container's status to traverse the container's lifecycle using the commands `docker container stop`, `docker container pause`, `docker container unpause`, `docker container start`, `docker container attach`, and `docker container start -a`.

- PORTS: It shows the ports that this container uses. We will talk about that in Chapter 4 later in the book.

- NAMES: Shows the nickname of the container. The Docker engine autogenerates a text name for the container, which you can use interchangeably with the container ID. This nickname is in the format adjective_noun. You can set the name that you want using the `--name` option in the run subcommand, for example, `docker container run alpine --name myfirstcontainer`.

- To clear this lab, remove the image using `docker image rm alpine`. Similarly, to remove the container, run `docker container rm d99b153cf127` or `docker container rm xenodochial_stonebraker`. You can concatenate several Docker commands together. For example, to remove all the images you have, use `docker image rm -f $(docker image ls -q)`. The `-f` option is to force removing the images because if there is a container based on an image, the Docker engine, by default, will refuse to remove this image. The `-q` option is for quiet mode. The Docker engine will execute the command in the brackets first; therefore, the output of `docker image ls -q` will be the input of `docker image rm -f`. Similarly, to remove all the containers that are on the host, use `docker container rm -f (docker container ls -aq)`.

Container Lifecycle

Let us try to control the container and change its status, as in Figure 3-4. In one terminal, try this:

```
docker container run -it --name test ubuntu /bin/bash
root@812ac3501f30:/# while true; do date;sleep 5;done
```

The -it stands for an interactive terminal to interact with the container and run commands inside it. They are from the run command options, and you can combine as many options as you want. The -it is the same as -i -t or -t -i or -ti.

In another terminal, try pausing this infinite loop of printing the date every 5 seconds:

```
docker container pause test
```

The first terminal will halt. Write docker container ls.

To unpause, write docker container unpause test.

To stop, use docker container stop test.

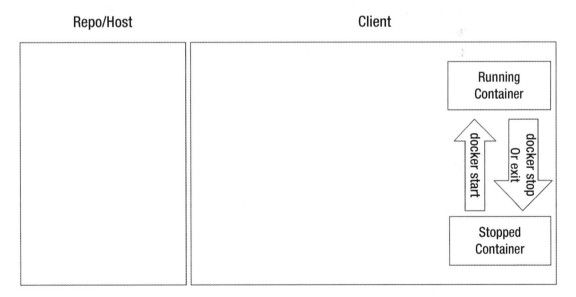

Figure 3-4. *Manage your container*

21

After you stopped the container, the container will exit and will not be running anymore. To verify that, run docker container ls. You will not find the test container in the list. Again, if you want to list the containers on your host, including the exited ones, run docker container run ls -a. test will be listed now. However, the container is still on your host and not deleted. To entirely remove it from the host, run docker container rm test. Rerun docker container ls -a. test has been removed now and is not listed in the output.

The last two most important commands to manage the container are detaching and attaching the container. To run the container in a daemon or detached mode, you use the -d option in the run subcommand. Type docker container run -d -it --name test1 ubuntu /bin/bash, as in Listing 3-3. A container ID will be displayed, and the shell will be back, but if you run docker container ls, you will find that the container test1 is running in the background. If you want to interact with it, you will need to attach the interactive terminal to it by running docker container attach test1. For example, let us install curl as a new layer inside the container. Type #apt-get update, #apt-get -y install curl. Now, we installed the curl package. The base image of ubuntu always stays intact. But to save your changes, you will need to commit this container as a new image, as we will see in the next section.

To exit the interactive mode, type exit. The container has stopped and is not running anymore. If you want to rerun in the background in detached mode, type docker container start test1. If you want to start it in an interactive mode, type docker container start -a test1. The -a option here stands for attach, so you start the container and attach it in one step. This last command is equivalent to two commands: docker container start test1 followed by docker container attach test1. If you want to exit the interactive mode but keep the container running in detached mode in the background without exiting it, use the **escape sequence: Ctrl+P and then Ctrl+Q**.

To know everything that has been executed in the container, you can use docker logs test1.

Figure 3-5 summarizes all the commands in the subsection and shows the container lifecycle.

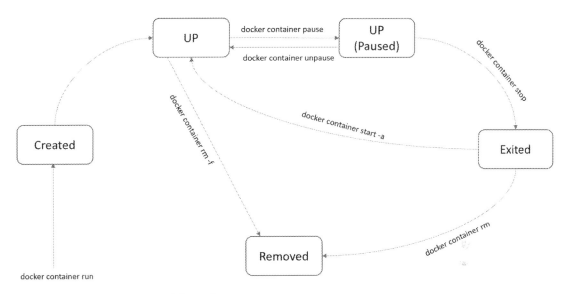

Figure 3-5. *Container lifecycle*

Create Your First Image

To commit this container into a new image, you can do it using the docker commit subcommand or by the Dockerfile, as in Figure 3-6. The Dockerfile is the more practical way in the real world. However, we shall see both ways.

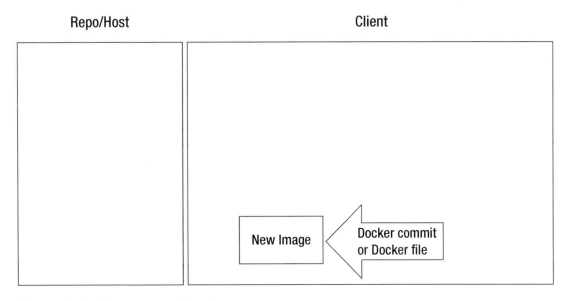

Figure 3-6. *Create your first image*

Using Commit

At the shell, type `docker container commit test1 testimage`. A new image will be created.

To check the image has been created, run `docker image ls`.

Listing 3-3. Install a package inside a container and commit it into a new image

```
$ docker container run -d -it --name test1 ubuntu /bin/bash
Unable to find image 'ubuntu:latest' locally
latest: Pulling from library/ubuntu
a31c7b29f4ad: Pull complete
Digest: sha256:b3e2e47d016c08b3396b5ebe06ab0b711c34e7f37b98c9d37abe79
4b71cea0a2
Status: Downloaded newer image for ubuntu:latest
50450d0d3643768ae6d7b4753a96c923866ddaca28f3fd204c249416c15e73fe
[node3] (local) root@192.168.0.16 ~
$ docker container ls
CONTAINER ID    IMAGE        COMMAND        CREATED         STATUS
PORTS        NAMES
50450d0d3643    ubuntu       "/bin/bash"    15 seconds ago   Up 13 seconds
             test1
[node3] (local) root@192.168.0.16 ~
$ docker container attach test1
root@50450d0d3643:/# apt-get update
Get:1 http://security.ubuntu.com/ubuntu focal-security InRelease [114 kB]
[truncated]
Get:18 http://archive.ubuntu.com/ubuntu focal-backports/universe amd64
Packages [6303 B]
Fetched 18.4 MB in 2s (7886 kB/s)
Reading package lists... Done
root@50450d0d3643:/# apt-get install curl
Reading package lists... Done
Building dependency tree
Reading state information... Done
The following additional packages will be installed:
```

```
  ca-certificates krb5-locales libasn1-8-heimdal libbrotli1 [truncated]
  libsqlite3-0 libssh-4 libssl1.1 libwind0-heimdal openssl publicsuffix
0 upgraded, 32 newly installed, 0 to remove and 0 not upgraded.
Need to get 5445 kB of archives.
After this operation, 16.7 MB of additional disk space will be used.
Do you want to continue? [Y/n] y
Get:1 http://archive.ubuntu.com/ubuntu focal-updates/main amd64 libssl1.1
amd64 1.1.1f-1ubuntu2.4 [1319 kB]
[truncated]
Setting up curl (7.68.0-1ubuntu2.5) ...
Processing triggers for libc-bin (2.31-0ubuntu9.2) ...
Processing triggers for ca-certificates (20210119~20.04.1) ...
Updating certificates in /etc/ssl/certs...
0 added, 0 removed; done.
Running hooks in /etc/ca-certificates/update.d...
done.
root@50450d0d3643:/# exit
exit
[node3] (local) root@192.168.0.16 ~
$ docker container commit test1 testimage
sha256:46e21a42b3cc374a43047527c6050832d25f6addbc2698d359355ed9687da2ae
[node3] (local) root@192.168.0.16 ~
$ docker image ls
REPOSITORY    TAG       IMAGE ID      CREATED          SIZE
testimage     latest    46e21a42b3cc  40 seconds ago   118MB
ubuntu        latest    c29284518f49  27 hours ago     72.8MB
```

Using Dockerfile

Creating an image from a container using the Dockerfile is merely two steps:

- Write the Dockerfile.

- Build the Dockerfile.

To verify that the image has been built and created, you list the images. To confirm that your changes are engraved in the image, run the new image into a new container. Let us have a step-by-step example.

- Open your text editor (e.g., vi or nano on Ubuntu or Notepad on Windows) and write the code in Listing 3-4.

Listing 3-4. Create your first Dockerfile

```
FROM ubuntu:latest
RUN apt-get update && apt-get install curl -y
```

- Save as Dockerfile with uppercase D and with no extension, for example, vi Dockerfile, as in Listing 3-5.

We will build the image using the following command, `docker image build -t testimagedockerfile .`, as in Listing 3-5, with the `build` subcommand. The `-t` is to add a tag to the image, and the `.` at the end indicates that it is at the current path and not a subdirectory.

Listing 3-5. Build the Dockerfile

```
[node4] (local) root@192.168.0.15 ~
$ vi Dockerfile
[node4] (local) root@192.168.0.15 ~
$ docker image build -t testimagedockerfile .
Sending build context to Docker daemon    47MB
Step 1/2 : FROM ubuntu:latest
 ---> c29284518f49
Step 2/2 : RUN apt-get update && apt-get install curl -y
 ---> Running in e5f44b8a41c9
Get:1 http://security.ubuntu.com/ubuntu focal-security InRelease [114 kB]
[truncated]
Running hooks in /etc/ca-certificates/update.d...
done.
Removing intermediate container e5f44b8a41c9
 ---> 849ccbc12892
Successfully built 849ccbc12892
Successfully tagged testimagedockerfile:latest
[node4] (local) root@192.168.0.15 ~
```

```
$ docker image ls
REPOSITORY              TAG        IMAGE ID        CREATED             SIZE
testimagedockerfile     latest     849ccbc12892    About a minute ago  118MB
ubuntu                  latest     c29284518f49    27 hours ago        72.8MB
[node4] (local) root@192.168.0.15 ~
$ docker container run -it testimagedockerfile
root@ba9d24780c10:/# which curl
/usr/bin/curl
root@ba9d24780c10:/# exit
exit
```

A path should be displayed indicating that curl is installed in ubuntu. To know any image layers that you download, use docker history testimagedockerfile.

Note   If you build the image without specifying a tag to it by using docker image build ., the image will be an unnamed image, which is called a dangled image. You can later name it by using docker image tag <image ID> . To remove all the dangled images, use docker image prune.

Push Your Images

This step is our final one in the Docker flow, as in Figure 3-7. Now, after you create your images, you should push them to the repository. In our case, we will use Docker Hub as our repo. There are plenty of others, and you can create your own local registry. If you are using Docker EE, the DTR is your local registry. You can create a free account at Docker Hub at http://hub.docker.com and push your images there. They will be available for public use as well.

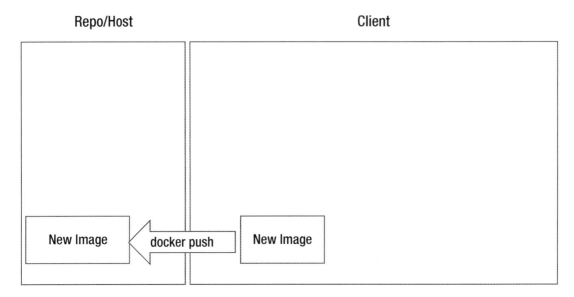

Figure 3-7. *Push your images*

To push your images successfully, they must contain your username at Docker Hub. Therefore, we need to rename your image using the docker image tag testimagedockerfile <your username>/testimagedockerfile subcommand, as in Listing 3-6. Then type docker login and enter your Docker username and password. After you log in successfully, run docker image push <your username>/testimagedockerfile. Open in the browser the Docker Hub website, refresh, and find your image pushed correctly, as in Figure 3-8. Do the same for the testimage image as well.

Listing 3-6. Push your image to Docker Hub

```
$ docker image tag testimagedockerfile engyfouda/testimagedockerfile
[node4] (local) root@192.168.0.15 ~
$ docker image ls
REPOSITORY                         TAG      IMAGE ID      CREATED         SIZE
engyfouda/testimagedockerfile      latest   849ccbc12892  11 minutes ago  118MB
testimagedockerfile                latest   849ccbc12892  11 minutes ago   118MB
ubuntu                             latest   c29284518f49  27 hours ago    72.8MB
[node4] (local) root@192.168.0.15 ~
$ docker login
```

Login with your Docker ID to push and pull images from Docker Hub. If you
don't have a Docker ID, head over to https://hub.docker.com to create one.
Username: engyfouda
Password:
Login Succeeded
[node4] (local) root@192.168.0.15 ~
$ docker image push engyfouda/testimagedockerfile
Using default tag: latest
The push refers to repository [docker.io/engyfouda/testimagedockerfile]
7e0a236b04b9: Pushed
a70daca533d0: Mounted from library/ubuntu
latest: digest: sha256:b2f94dcb21a700c9a87b3721abd4ffd4b14869782307d672
3d7529488dd80e15 size: 741

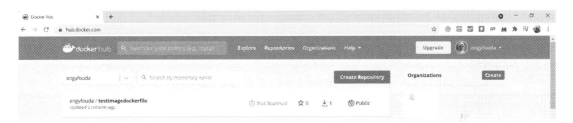

Figure 3-8. *Check your image at Docker Hub*

Dockerfile Commands

The Dockerfile is a text file and not case sensitive. However, the convention is to write the
commands in all caps. Some instructions create new layers, while others add metadata
to the image.

- Examples of instructions that create new layers: FROM, RUN, COPY.

- Example of instructions that add metadata: EXPOSE, WORKDIR, ENV,
  ENTRYPOINT.

This section will focus on the instructions that appear in the DCA exam and not
on all the instructions that you can use in a Dockerfile. You can consult the Docker
documentation if you need more details.

The FROM Instruction

- You must start your Dockerfile with a FROM instruction to set the base image. If you want to create a new image with no parent image, use FROM scratch.

- You can use it any number of times, as we will see later in the multistage build.

- Example: FROM ubuntu

The MAINTAINER Instruction

- This is a metadata instruction to indicate the Dockerfile author's contact.

- Example: MAINTAINER Engy <efoda@ieee.org>

The COPY Instruction

- This instruction is used to copy files and directories from your local host to be engraved inside the container.

- Example: COPY test /newdir/test

The ADD Instruction

The differences between COPY and ADD instructions are tricky questions that you will almost always have in the DCA exam. Here are the differences:

- ADD supports URL handling, while COPY does not do that.

- ADD supports extra features like local-only tar extraction.

- ADD supports regular expression handling, while COPY does not.

- Example: ADD http://www.mysite.com/file.tar.gz/code/source

The ENV Instruction

- This instruction sets the environment variables in the container, for example, setting a log path other than the long one that the Docker engine sets by default.

- Example: `ENV log_dir /var/log`

The USER Instruction

- By default, the Docker engine will set the container's user to root, which can be harmful. Actually, no one gives root privileges like that. Therefore, you should set a user ID and username to your container.

- Example: `USER 75 engy`

The WORKDIR Instruction

- You use WORKDIR to set your active directory.

- The tricky question that comes here is that the paths provided in the WORKDIR instructions will concatenate. Let us clarify that with an example.

- Example:

```
WORKDIR /var
WORKDIR source
RUN apt-get update
```

- The RUN instruction will be executed in the path of /var/source.

The VOLUME Instruction

- The VOLUME instruction creates a directory in the image filesystem, which can later be used for mounting volumes from the Docker host or the other containers. We will talk about that in detail in Chapter 5.

- Example: `VOLUME vol`

The EXPOSE Instruction

- This instruction is to make the container port accessible from the browser, outside the container, so that the world can send requests to the container services. We will talk about that in detail in Chapter 4.

- You can specify multiple ports in a single line.

- By default, the Docker engine will assign TCP as your protocol.

- Example: EXPOSE 8081 80/udp

- This example will expose port 8081 as a TCP port and 80 as UDP.

The RUN Instruction

- RUN is one of the most used instructions in the Dockerfile. You use it to install any packages as a new layer inside the image during the build time. For example, your application needs to update ubuntu and then install curl.

- In such case, your Dockerfile will look like this:

```
FROM ubuntu
RUN apt-get update && apt-get install curl
```

The CMD Instruction

Again, you might get a question asking about the difference between the RUN and CMD instructions. Here are the differences:

- As we have seen in an example earlier, the CMD is executed when you run a container from your image, while the RUN instruction, as we mentioned, is executed during the build time of the image.

- You can have only one CMD instruction in a Dockerfile. If you add more, only the last one takes effect, while you can have as many RUN instructions as you need in the same Dockerfile.

- You can add a health check to the CMD instruction, for example, `HEALTHCHECK CMD curl --fail http://localhost/health || exit 1`, which tells the Docker engine to kill the container with exit status 1 if the container health fails.

- The CMD syntax uses this form ["param", param", "param"] when used in conjunction with the ENTRYPOINT instruction. It should be in the following form CMD ["executable", "param1", "param2"...] if used by itself.

- Example: `CMD "echo" "Hello World!"`

The ENTRYPOINT Instruction

- To instantly run an executable command when a container is crafted from an image, use the ENTRYPOINT instruction.

- Again, you can receive a tricky question about ENTRYPOINT and CMD; remember that ENTRYPOINT overrides the CMD instruction, and CMD's parameters are used as arguments to ENTRYPOINT.

- For example, you have a Dockerfile that has the following two instructions:

```
CMD "This is my container"
ENTRYPOINT echo
```

- When you run a container from this image, the Docker engine will execute it as `ENTRYPOINT echo "This is my container"` and will print `This is my container`.

The inspect Command

You can use the inspect subcommand to get all the details of any object in Docker. The exam focuses on the `--filter` and `--format` options. These options are also options in the `docker image ls` command.

Let us try inspecting your testimage; run docker image inspect testimage. The output is too long, as you see, and it consists of sections and subsections. If you want a specific value, you add them in sequence after the --format option. For example, to get the architecture and operating system an image is compatible with, you run docker image inspect –format='{{.Architecture}} {{.Os}}' <image-id>. The Architecture is the section, where the OS is a subsection inside it.

An example for the --filter option is to filter the dangled images only. You can do that by running docker image ls --filter dangling=true.

Multistage Build

The primary purpose of multistage image build is optimizing images by copying artifacts selectively from previous stages to keep the image small. The Dockerfile, in this case, will contain more than one FROM instruction. You can name your stages as well.

Here is an example of a multistage Dockerfile where the first stage is named:

```
FROM golang:1.16 AS builder
WORKDIR /go/src/github.com/alexellis/href-counter/
RUN go get -d -v golang.org/x/net/html
COPY app.go     .
RUN CGO_ENABLED=0 GOOS=linux go build -a -installsuffix cgo -o app .

FROM alpine:latest
RUN apk --no-cache add ca-certificates
WORKDIR /root/
COPY --from=builder /go/src/github.com/alexellis/href-counter/app .
CMD ["./app"]
```

The previous example is from the Docker documentation at the following link: https://docs.docker.com/develop/develop-images/multistage-build/.

Summary

This chapter discussed in detail the Docker flow and the container lifecycle. These concepts are the cornerstone to understand and work with Docker. Moreover, it discussed a crucial concept of how to optimize the images and decrease their size using multistage build.

CHAPTER 4

Networking

In this chapter, you will learn about networking and how containers can communicate despite being isolated by default. The isolation protects containers from one of them logging in inside the other and messing it up. Moreover, containers are isolated from the Internet by default. You will learn how containers can communicate with each other and with hosts and make their services available on the Internet.

Therefore, the chapter will cover the following topics:

- Networking in the Docker Community Edition (CE) using the bridge network

- Swarm networking using the overlay network

- Kubernetes networking foundation

Containers' Isolated Networking

From the powerful security features of Docker is isolating various namespaces. In this chapter, we will focus on the networking namespace only. The model relies on that every container has its own network stack and resources isolated in a sandbox. *Sandbox* means isolating the container from the Internet, networks, and other containers by default. The sandbox includes Ethernet interfaces, ports, routing tables, and DNS config.

Every time a container is created, it is assigned a unique IP. You can get this IP by inspecting the container using `docker container inspect <Container Name or ID>` and scrolling to `Network Settings` or by adding the format option: `docker inspect --format='{{.NetworkSettings.IPAddress}}' <Container Name/ID>`.

By default, the container is connected to the bridge network unless specified to be connected to a user-defined network. To list the networks, run `docker network ls`, as in Figure 4-1.

© Engy Fouda 2022
E. Fouda, *A Complete Guide to Docker for Operations and Development*,
https://doi.org/10.1007/978-1-4842-8117-8_4

```
$ docker network ls
NETWORK ID         NAME         DRIVER       SCOPE
902ddb194ae4       bridge       bridge       local
e938770ab965       host         host         local
becec05992fc       none         null         local
```

Figure 4-1. *List the networks*

If you run the preceding command on a Docker Community Edition (CE), the Docker engine will create the preceding three networks for you by default: bridge, host, and none.

- none: The loopback (lo) interface for local communication within a container.

- host: The container gets attached to the host network stack and shares the host's IP addresses and ports.

- bridge: The default network if the network is not configured using the --net option of the docker run subcommand.

Since the containers are isolated by default, they communicate using the endpoints/virtual Ethernet interfaces where the packets transfer over the docker0 network. The docker0 acts as a switch allowing the frames between the containers and the external network, as in Figure 4-2.

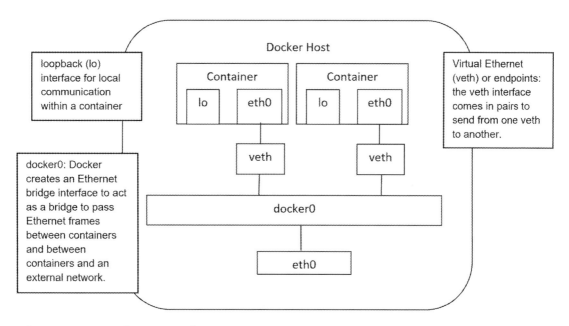

Figure 4-2. *Bridge network*

User-Defined Bridge Network

You can group your containers into user-defined private networks. You explicitly choose which container can connect to which. For example, you have four containers. Two of them are connected to the user-defined network called mynet, one is connected to the default bridge network, and one is common between the two networks, mynet and docker0, as in Figure 4-3.

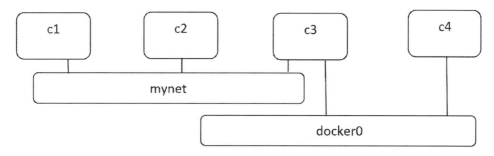

Figure 4-3. *User-defined network*

To define the four containers, run Listing 4-1. In Listing 4-1, to create a new user-defined bridge network, you use the `docker network create` subcommand and specify the `driver` as `bridge`. To connect a container to a network, use `docker network connect`. Create the container with the `-itd` options for interactive terminal daemon mode. Use `--net` or `--network` to specify the network and `--name` to name the containers. The image used is `ubuntu,` and `bash` is the command. Now, the four containers are running in the background in the daemon mode.

Next, inspect the two networks, mynet and bridge, to get the containers' IPs. As mentioned before, you can also get the containers' IPs by inspecting each one of them.

Attach to c3 and install the ping utility inside this container as this latest image – up until writing this book – does not have it installed. You update the kernel and install the ping using `apt-get update && apt-get install -y iputils-ping`.

Now, ping each of the other containers by sending two packets using the option of `-c 2` followed by the container name or IP. Either the name or IP will work with c1, c2, and c3 because they are connected to a user-defined network.

However, pinging with the name will not work with c4 because it is connected to a bridge network. Ping it with its IP. It will work correctly. This is a difference between the default bridge network and the user-defined one. Try to repeat the same with the other containers. Click the escape sequence: `Ctrl+P` followed by `Ctrl+Q`. The shell prompt will show while the container is still running in the daemon mode. If you exited the container using the `exit` command, you need to start the container before proceeding. To start the container, run `docker start <container name/ID>`.

If you attach to c2, for example, it will be able to ping c1 and c3 with the name or IP but will not be able to ping c4 at all because they are not grouped on the same network. Similarly, c1 will not be able to reach c4, not by name or IP.

In conclusion, c3, which is connected to the two networks, can connect to all the other containers on the user-defined network and to c4, as they are connected on the default bridge network.

Listing 4-1. User-defined network example

```
$ docker network create --driver bridge mynet
$ docker run -itd --net mynet --name c1 ubuntu bash
$ docker run -itd --net mynet --name c2 ubuntu bash
$ docker run -itd --net mynet --name c3 ubuntu bash
$ docker run -itd --name c4 ubuntu bash
```

```
$ docker network connect bridge c3

$ docker container ls
CONTAINER ID   IMAGE    COMMAND    CREATED       STATUS        PORTS NAMES
90eba8eced2b   ubuntu   "bash"     2 hours ago   Up 2 hours          c4
7a78595543fd   ubuntu   "bash"     2 hours ago   Up 2 hours          c3
d2a4afbe0a72   ubuntu   "bash"     2 hours ago   Up 2 hours          c2
2a7204098f1c   ubuntu   "bash"     2 hours ago   Up 2 hours          c1
$docker network inspect mynet
--truncated–
        "Containers": {
            "2a7204098f1c3d7691b7266197f0b490322eec1e6d94034d22eea92
            4be9e7f45": {
                "Name": "c1",
                "EndpointID": "fddc539c7509129c635092e2efce7f39163b8
                bea0de8a5652d2d993e49d8230e",
                "MacAddress": "02:42:ac:13:00:02",
                "IPv4Address": "172.19.0.2/16",
                "IPv6Address": ""
            },
            "7a78595543fd104ac684b96ebe3b6f8be3a342ca738ae45b8ca019e
            a1698b0f6": {
                "Name": "c3",
                "EndpointID": "e6076bf274887966a41b8e4a445d73c048ddc
                671be2199d73a1c61d7981a4b00",
                "MacAddress": "02:42:ac:13:00:04",
                "IPv4Address": "172.19.0.4/16",
                "IPv6Address": ""
            },
            "d2a4afbe0a72c0cacdebb262cf0f62058f9a9ad161705013533a179
            579d803eb": {
                "Name": "c2",
                "EndpointID": "a67ef9cce48bed6d6126745298e1ce23a9e1f8
                ab5d2d2de2034095ea353ab88f",
                "MacAddress": "02:42:ac:13:00:03",
                "IPv4Address": "172.19.0.3/16",
```

```
                "IPv6Address": ""
        }

$docker network inspect bridge
--truncated--
        "Containers": {
            "7a78595543fd104ac684b96ebe3b6f8be3a342ca738ae45b8ca019ea
            1698b0f6": {
                "Name": "c3",
                "EndpointID": "c4112d7b0eaca58d2874b7fa2e4e3bc9551eb
                b2f4bc316ff9d44b506cbdb03c2",
                "MacAddress": "02:42:ac:11:00:03",
                "IPv4Address": "172.17.0.3/16",
                "IPv6Address": ""
            },
            "90eba8eced2be1396c8817a1a686cd3481950c320fb232617e40cf827
            5dccc04": {
                "Name": "c4",
                "EndpointID": "d308c8a316569c3f123c51c4f5725cadbaafc695
                6ea25cc658039a05a88ead6a",
                "MacAddress": "02:42:ac:11:00:02",
                "IPv4Address": "172.17.0.2/16",
                "IPv6Address": ""
            }

$docker attach c3
# apt-get update && apt-get install -y iputils-ping
#ping -c 2 c1
PING c1 (172.19.0.2) 56(84) bytes of data.
64 bytes from c1.mynet (172.19.0.2): icmp_seq=1 ttl=64 time=0.177 ms
64 bytes from c1.mynet (172.19.0.2): icmp_seq=2 ttl=64 time=0.124 ms

--- c1 ping statistics ---
2 packets transmitted, 2 received, 0% packet loss, time 999ms
rtt min/avg/max/mdev = 0.124/0.150/0.177/0.026 ms
#ping -c 2 c2
PING c2 (172.19.0.3) 56(84) bytes of data.
```

```
64 bytes from d2a4afbe0a72 (172.19.0.3): icmp_seq=1 ttl=64 time=0.061 ms
64 bytes from d2a4afbe0a72 (172.19.0.3): icmp_seq=2 ttl=64 time=0.061 ms

--- c2 ping statistics ---
2 packets transmitted, 2 received, 0% packet loss, time 999ms
rtt min/avg/max/mdev = 0.061/0.061/0.061/0.000 ms

#ping -c 2 c4
ping: c4: No address associated with hostname

#ping -c 2 <c4 IP>
root@7a78595543fd:/# ping -c 2 172.17.0.2
PING 172.17.0.2 (172.17.0.2) 56(84) bytes of data.
64 bytes from 172.17.0.2: icmp_seq=1 ttl=64 time=0.196 ms
64 bytes from 172.17.0.2: icmp_seq=2 ttl=64 time=0.117 ms

--- 172.17.0.2 ping statistics ---
2 packets transmitted, 2 received, 0% packet loss, time 1000ms
rtt min/avg/max/mdev = 0.117/0.156/0.196/0.039 ms
```

Exposing Container Ports

In the previous section, you learned how the containers can communicate with each other. In this section, you will learn how the services inside the containers can be accessed from outside hosts. This is done by exposing the container ports. There are two ways to expose the container services and make the port mapping:

1. Bind using the –p or --publish option with the run command at the command line.

2. Expose the port in the Dockerfile and use the –P option afterward.

An example of the -p option is docker run -d -p 80 nginx. In such case, the Docker engine will bind port 80 inside the container to a random valid port at the host. Hence, the container's service will be exposed and can be accessed. To find the port bindings, use docker container ls -a. Under the PORTS column, you will find the generated host port and the container port that you assigned. Also, you can use docker port <container name/ID> or $docker inspect --format='{{.NetworkSettings. Ports}}' <container name/ID>, as in Listing 4-2.

In the example, the Docker engine generated port 49153. It is the host port bound to port 80 inside the `nginx` container. You can specify the host port to 81 as in the `nginx1` container, and do not leave it to the engine by using `-p 81:81`. However, if you do, you must keep track of the host ports you assign. If you assign a used host port to any other container, the new container will fail because the port is already bound. You can access the `nginx` service that is running inside the container by typing `http://localhost:81` in any browser.

For this `-p` option, the complete syntax is `<IP>:<Host Port>:<Container Port>`. However, the container port is the only mandatory parameter; the IP and the host port are optional. Therefore, we can find all these variant examples:

- `docker run -p 195.23.0.15:80:80` (where you specified the IP, host port, and container port)

- `docker run -p 80:80` (where you specified the host port and the container port; the IP will be 0.0.0.0, which means that it is publicly accessible)

- `docker run -p 80` (where you specified the container port only and left the engine to generate a free host port for you; the IP will be 0.0.0.0)

- `docker run -p 195.23.0.15::80` (where you specified the IP and the container port; the daemon will generate the host port for you)

Listing 4-2. Container port binding

```
$ docker run -d --name nginx -p 80 nginx
f9ed674b9790a6eef02416de3f8cede65b62a60179ef054919addafd9b7f472c

$ docker container ls -a
CONTAINER ID    IMAGE     COMMAND                   CREATED
    STATUS                    PORTS                 NAMES
f9ed674b9790    nginx     "/docker-entrypoint...."  2 seconds ago
    Up Less than a second     0.0.0.0:49153->80/tcp    nginx

$ docker port nginx
80/tcp -> 0.0.0.0:49153
$docker inspect --format='{{.NetworkSettings.Ports}}' nginx
map[80/tcp:[{0.0.0.0 49153}]]
```

```
$ docker run -d --name nginx1 -p 81:81 nginx
6f54b50dd1ac21f4df8d3969f33641ff3198ece3cbd8ed6802258864024f308e

$ docker container ls
CONTAINER ID   IMAGE   COMMAND                    CREATED
STATUS                  PORTS                     NAMES
6f54b50dd1ac   nginx   "/docker-entrypoint...."   1 second ago
Up Less than a second   80/tcp, 0.0.0.0:81->81/tcp   nginx1
f9ed674b9790   nginx   "/docker-entrypoint...."   4 seconds ago
Up 2 seconds            0.0.0.0:49153->80/tcp       nginx
```

Let us try the second way: the Dockerfile and -P option. We first create the Dockerfile. The second step is to build this Dockerfile into an image. The final step is to run a container based on this image with the -P option.

Now, run vi Dockerfile to write your Dockerfile. As mentioned in Chapter 3, *Dockerfile* must be without any extensions and must be with an uppercase D. You can use vi or nano or Notepad or any word processing software to write the Dockerfile, as in Listing 4-3.

Listing 4-3. The Dockerfile exposing the container's port

```
FROM nginx
EXPOSE 80
```

Now, as in Listing 4-4, build the image and name it nginx2, and do not forget the . at the end of the build subcommand to indicate that the Dockerfile is at the current path and not in a subdirectory. We will craft a container named nginx2 from this image using the -P option. You can expose more than one port in the same EXPOSE instruction in the Dockerfile. The -P option tells Docker to bind each exposed container port to a random port on the host's interface. Then list all the running containers that you have right now and inspect their host and container ports.

Listing 4-4. Expose the container's port in the Dockerfile

```
$ docker build -t nginx2 .
Sending build context to Docker daemon     47MB
Step 1/2 : from nginx
 ---> dd34e67e3371
Step 2/2 : expose 80
```

```
 ---> Running in d78648314b32
Removing intermediate container d78648314b32
 ---> 230c445ba6e9
Successfully built 230c445ba6e9
Successfully tagged nginx2:latest
```

```
$ docker run -d --name nginx2 -P nginx2
a5ee663cb23c47b73f12b796f02f4bafa9575e03217878cdbbfb23b6619fa6a9
```

```
$ docker container ls
CONTAINER ID    IMAGE      COMMAND                        CREATED
STATUS          PORTS                          NAMES
a5ee663cb23c    nginx2     "/docker-entrypoint...."    17 seconds ago
Up 16 seconds    0.0.0.0:49154->80/tcp          nginx2
6f54b50dd1ac    nginx      "/docker-entrypoint...."    25 minutes ago
Up 25 minutes    80/tcp, 0.0.0.0:81->81/tcp     nginx1
f9ed674b9790    nginx      "/docker-entrypoint...."    25 minutes ago
Up 25 minutes    0.0.0.0:49153->80/tcp          nginx
```

Some Differences in Networking Between Windows and Linux

If you are running the previous listings on Windows and not on Linux, you will find some differences:

- There are no bridge networks, as in Figure 4-4.

```
$ docker network ls
NETWORK ID          NAME            DRIVER          SCOPE
384fe1c44d0f        myswitch        transparent     local
45291ad0bcf7        nat             nat             local
0e69f8a789cf        none            null            local
```

Figure 4-4. *Networks on a Windows host*

- Localhost must be explicitly published. As Windows cannot resolve localhost, you cannot use http://localhost:81 as we did in the previous section. For more info, visit https://docs.docker.com/v17.09/docker-for-windows/#explore-the-application-and-run-examples.

- To access the site on the Windows Docker host, you need to make the request using the container's IP address using the `ipconfig` command, as in Figure 4-5. For more info, visit

  `https://blog.sixeyed.com/published-ports-on-windows-containers-dont-do-loopback/`

```
PS C:\Users\Administrator\firstapp> ipconfig

Windows IP Configuration


Ethernet adapter vEthernet (HNS Internal NIC):

   Connection-specific DNS Suffix  . :
   Link-local IPv6 Address . . . . . : fe80::984c:5b2b:492e:8aa4%5
   IPv4 Address. . . . . . . . . . . : 172.29.160.1
   Subnet Mask . . . . . . . . . . . : 255.255.240.0
   Default Gateway . . . . . . . . . :

Ethernet adapter vEthernet (myswitch):

   Connection-specific DNS Suffix  . :
   Link-local IPv6 Address . . . . . : fe80::dd74:de20:e89a:2ebc%7
   IPv4 Address. . . . . . . . . . . : 172.19.118.11
   Subnet Mask . . . . . . . . . . . : 255.255.224.0
   Default Gateway . . . . . . . . . : 172.19.96.1

Tunnel adapter isatap.{78FFED2B-0F8C-4495-98C1-A26E95C03A01}:

   Media State . . . . . . . . . . . : Media disconnected
   Connection-specific DNS Suffix  . :

Tunnel adapter isatap.{6E77B4EE-1457-45A9-84D5-BD9B667C8B88}:

   Media State . . . . . . . . . . . : Media disconnected
   Connection-specific DNS Suffix  . :
```

Figure 4-5. *Use ipconfig to get the container's IP*

In the second section of the output in Figure 4-5, in the switch Ethernet adapter information, check the IPv4 Address. You will find the IP, for example, 172.19.118.11. Assume that we are running a web application that counts the number of hits to a website. The application uses Python, Redis, and Flask. Now, use the IP in the browser instead of the localhost with the host port, as in Figure 4-6.

Figure 4-6. *Use the IP instead of the localhost*

Swarm Networking

In the previous sections, we mentioned three networks that the Docker CE creates by default, which are none, host, and bridge. They use null, host, and bridge drivers, respectively. These are not the only drivers available in Docker. There are also the overlay and macvlan drivers.

The networks that use the macvlan drivers add a MAC address to a container. Thus, it appears as a physical device on the network, and Docker routes the packets using the MAC addresses.

In this section, we will focus on the networks that use the overlay driver. When you initialize a swarm, Docker creates an ingress network that uses the overlay driver by default for you. You can create your user-defined overlay networks as well. You use the overlay network when you need a distributed network among multiple Docker daemon hosts, where you need multiple containers at different hosts to communicate. Also, you need it when you have swarm services interacting with each other.

Let us have an example. First, we will build a simple swarm of one manager node and one worker node. We can use Docker playground, https://labs.play-with-docker.com, to do this hands-on lab. On the left panel, click CREATE NEW INSTANCE twice to create node1 and node2. We will set node1 as the manager by running $docker swarm init --advertise-addr <Node IP>. You can get the node IP from the top of the page. A long token will be generated if you want to add a worker to the swarm, as in Listing 4-5. This long generated token is one of Docker's security features as well.

Listing 4-5. Initialize a swarm

```
$ docker swarm init --advertise-addr 192.168.0.8
Swarm initialized: current node (ovkaxux7f04vt74sc3hduj8vk) is now a
manager.
```

To add a worker to this swarm, run the following command:

```
docker swarm join --token SWMTKN-1-47hqnq5eivhk6g1jk9owyt4tuy7y9v8p8p4
co0loaie7z6mys2-5wkplsmi7hlrwbfig67ly43yx 192.168.0.8:2377
```

To add a manager to this swarm, run 'docker swarm join-token manager' and follow the instructions.

To add a worker, copy this command $docker swarm join with the long token. To copy and paste on Docker playground, you use Ctrl+Insert to copy and Shift+Insert to paste. Paste this command on node2 to make it join the swarm as a worker, as follows:

```
$ docker swarm join --token SWMTKN-1-47hqnq5eivhk6g1jk9owyt4tuy7y9v8p8p4co0
loaie7z6mys2-5wkplsmi7hlrwbfig67ly43yx 192.168.0.8:2377
This node joined a swarm as a worker.
```

Now, return to node1 and list the nodes, as in Listing 4-6. List the nodes and observe the MANAGER STATUS. You will find one has Leader and the other is empty, indicating that we have one manager node, which is the leader as well, and one worker. Then we will create a new network called mynet that uses the overlay driver. Next, we will create a service that runs on the swarm that exposes port 80:80 and creates two replicas of the service running on the two nodes of the swarm.

Therefore, as you see, the manager node takes an additional task of scheduling and load-balancing in addition to assigning tasks to itself as it does to the rest of the swarm nodes.

Listing 4-6. Overlay hands-on lab

```
$ docker node ls
ID                                 HOSTNAME    STATUS    AVAILABILITY
    MANAGER STATUS    ENGINE VERSION
ovkaxux7f04vt74sc3hduj8vk *    node1       Ready     Active
    Leader           20.10.0
7gjlk7nbtc324n95d5rr5o5ze      node2       Ready     Active
                 20.10.0
[node1] (local) root@192.168.0.8 ~
$ docker network create -d overlay mynet
7ga090ot7f092ptmz55axn1z9
[node1] (local) root@192.168.0.8 ~
```

```
$ docker service create --name nginx --network mynet --publish published=80,
target=80,mode=host --replicas 2 nginx
7a05l9x2stuz50e7haz0ahwax
overall progress: 2 out of 2 tasks
1/2: running   [==================================================>]
2/2: running   [==================================================>]
verify: Service converged
[node1] (local) root@192.168.0.8 ~
$ docker service ls
ID              NAME         MODE         REPLICAS    IMAGE           PORTS
7a05l9x2stuz    nginx        replicated   2/2         nginx:latest
[node1] (local) root@192.168.0.8 ~
$ docker service ps nginx
ID              NAME         IMAGE          NODE       DESIRED STATE
CURRENT STATE               ERROR      PORTS
jekdowhdp01w    nginx.1      nginx:latest   node1      Running
Running 5 seconds ago       *:80->80/tcp
m1fihs281x21    nginx.2      nginx:latest   node2      Running
Running 5 seconds ago       *:80->80/tcp
```

Now, let's scale up to five replicas. Docker playground allows only five instances. Always the best practice is to use an odd number of managers. Therefore, our new cluster will be three managers and two workers. Create three more instances – node3, node4, and node5 – by clicking CREATE NEW INSTANCE. Again, on node1, run Listing 4-7.

Listing 4-7. Swarm join commands

```
$ docker swarm join-token manager
To add a manager to this swarm, run the following command:

    docker swarm join --token SWMTKN-1-47hqnq5eivhk6g1jk9owyt4tuy7y9v8p
    8p4co0loaie7z6mys2-237avlt7d2vdu351a5mkrv8lm 192.168.0.8:2377

[node1] (local) root@192.168.0.8 ~
$ docker swarm join-token worker
To add a worker to this swarm, run the following command:

    docker swarm join --token SWMTKN-1-47hqnq5eivhk6g1jk9owyt4tuy7y9v8p8p4
    co0loaie7z6mys2-5wkplsmi7hlrwbfig67ly43yx 192.168.0.8:2377
```

Run the generated manager token on node3 and node4. Run the worker token instruction on node5. So we will have node1, node3, and node4 as managers and node2 and node5 as workers. On node1, list the nodes again, as in Listing 4-8. The list shows the five nodes, with node1 as Leader, node3 and node4 as Reachable managers, and node2 and node5 as workers. Now scale up the service to five replicas by running `docker service scale nginx=5` on node1. You can also use `docker service update --replicas=5 nginx` to scale up the number of services.

Listing 4-8. Scaling up the service replicas to five

```
$ docker node ls
ID                             HOSTNAME    STATUS    AVAILABILITY
MANAGER STATUS    ENGINE VERSION
ovkaxux7f04vt74sc3hduj8vk *    node1       Ready     Active
Leader            20.10.0
7gjlk7nbtc324n95d5rr5o5ze      node2       Ready     Active
                  20.10.0
y31zv4hne3649e7ehu6teuezp      node3       Ready     Active
Reachable         20.10.0
w8h9gs7vr3egfatlvxy96iwfx      node4       Ready     Active
Reachable         20.10.0
36iorue55dunpszh7xc8tkmjp      node5       Ready     Active
                  20.10.0

$docker service scale nginx=5
nginx scaled to 5
overall progress: 5 out of 5 tasks
1/5: running   [==================================================>]
2/5: running   [==================================================>]
3/5: running   [==================================================>]
4/5: running   [==================================================>]
5/5: running   [==================================================>]
$ docker service ps nginx
ID              NAME       IMAGE          NODE      DESIRED STATE
CURRENT STATE              ERROR          PORTS
jekdowhdp01w    nginx.1    nginx:latest   node1     Running
Running 43 minutes ago        *:80->80/tcp
```

```
m1fihs281x21    nginx.2    nginx:latest    node2    Running
Running 43 minutes ago        *:80->80/tcp
qunzv1l30dbe    nginx.3    nginx:latest    node3    Running
Running about a minute ago    *:80->80/tcp
thitxktooge8    nginx.4    nginx:latest    node4    Running
Running about a minute ago    *:80->80/tcp
tisjgp4p4lcy    nginx.5    nginx:latest    node5    Running
Running about a minute ago    *:80->80/tcp
[node1] (local) root@192.168.0.8 ~
$ docker service rm nginx
nginx
[node1] (local) root@192.168.0.8 ~
$ docker network rm mynet
mynet
```

What Is the Best Number of Managers?

- Three or five or seven managers. Why?

  Think of it as a voting process. If we have an even number of four, where two voted for YES while the other two voted for NO, you will have a split-brain case and will not be able to decide. In other words, neither side holds the quorum/majority.

- You do not want more than seven, as the time taken to achieve consensus will be longer.

- Swarm managers have native support for high availability (HA).

- This means one or more managers can fail and the other managers will keep the swarm running.

- Managers are either leaders or followers. This is Raft terminology.

- An N-manager cluster tolerates the loss of at most $(N - 1)/2$ managers.

Datacenter Topology

To achieve optimal fault tolerance, be careful with the datacenter topology as well. Distribute manager nodes across a minimum of three availability zones to support HA. For more information, please check the Swarm Administration Guide at `https://docs.docker.com/engine/swarm/admin_guide/`.

Total manager nodes	Repartition (on three availability zones)
3	1-1-1
5	2-2-1
7	3-2-2
9	3-3-3

Exam question: This is almost a must-have question in the DCA exam.

When seven managers are in a swarm cluster, how would they be distributed across three datacenters or availability zones?

Choose 3-2-2.

Replicated vs. Global Services

- Replicated: The default replication mode of a service that will deploy a desired number of replicas and distribute them as evenly as possible across the cluster.

- Global: Runs a single replica on every node in the swarm. To deploy a global service, you need to pass the `--mode global` flag to the docker service create command.

Port Publishing Modes

- Ingress: The default mode of publishing a port on every node in the swarm, even nodes not running service replicas.

- Host: Publishes the service on swarm nodes running replicas only.

One of the popular DCA questions: What command ensures that overlay traffic between service tasks is encrypted?

Answer: `$docker network create -d overlay -o encrypted=true <network-name>`

Kubernetes Networking

The networking in Kubernetes is a little bit different. Kubernetes uses a service to provide a static interface to the deployments, where the pods are running. Services provide three main criteria:

1. Stable IP

2. DNS

3. Port

There are three types of services. Think of them as a stack upon each other, as in Figure 4-7. The ClusterIP is to provide the service inside the cluster. The NodePort is to make the service accessible from outside the cluster. The LoadBalancer is for integrating the cloud providers.

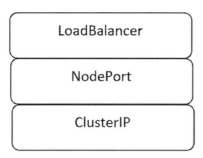

Figure 4-7. *Kubernetes services*

- A ClusterIP service has a stable IP address and port that is only accessible from inside the cluster. It registers a DNS name, a virtual IP, and a port with the cluster DNS.

- A NodePort service builds on top of ClusterIP and enables access from outside of the cluster. It adds a new port called NodePort to be used to reach the service from outside the cluster.

- A LoadBalancer service builds on top of the NodePort and integrates with load balancers from your cloud provider, for example, Azure.

The services are defined in YAML files, as in Listing 4-9. This service routes request traffic sent on port 8080 to port 80 in a pod with the label app nginx.

Listing 4-9. ClusterIP YAML example

```
apiVersion:  v1
kind:  Service
metadata:
  name:  app
spec:
  type:  clusterIP
  selector:
    app:  nginx
    ports:
    - port:  8080
      targetPort:  80
    -port:  4515
      targetPort:  443
```

Summary

Networking is a crucial concept in Docker and Kubernetes. This chapter discussed how the containers communicate in stand-alone and overlay networking. Since the DCA exam focuses on swarm and Kubernetes orchestrators, the chapter included both as well.

CHAPTER 5

Storage and Volumes

In this chapter, you will learn about storage and mounting volumes for stateful Docker containers and Kubernetes pods. For the Docker containers, there are two types of volumes, the persistent and the ephemeral. Also, there is a data volume. Moreover, there is a crucial difference between saving the data on volumes and using the filesystem when committing the containers to images.

Therefore, the chapter will cover the following topics:

- How to create a persistent volume for a stateful container and how to remove the container with the volume

- The ephemeral volumes shared between containers

- Data volume

- Filesystem vs. volumes

- Kubernetes volumes

Persistent Volumes

You can easily create a volume with any container by adding the option `-v` or `--volume` to the `docker run` command, as in Listing 5-1. Also, you can mount any needed volumes by adding the `VOLUME` command in the Dockerfile and in the docker-compose YAML file. Another way is to define volumes with services. In this section, we will show the first two ways of the `-v` option with the `docker run` subcommand and the `Dockerfile`.

In Listing 5-1, we try the first method of using the -v option, where the Docker daemon automatically creates the volumes for us when crafting the container from the image `ubuntu`. In this example, we named our container `test` to make it easier for us to follow instead of using the container ID. However, you can use the container's name and the ID interchangeably.

© Engy Fouda 2022
E. Fouda, *A Complete Guide to Docker for Operations and Development*,
https://doi.org/10.1007/978-1-4842-8117-8_5

To verify that the volume has been created, we use docker inspect --format='{{. Config.Volumes}}' <container name or ID>; the volume name will be displayed. To get the volume ID, we use docker inspect --format='{{.Mounts}}' <container name or ID>. All the information of the container volume will be displayed, as well as the paths on the host and inside the container and if its read/write flag equals true or not.

From the host, we can get the volumes created by using docker volume ls; the volume ID will be displayed in the list. The final step is to remove the container with the volume using docker rm -v <container name or ID>. Re-list the volumes using docker volume ls; the list will be empty if there are no other containers running.

Listing 5-1. Using the -v option in the docker run subcommand

```
$ docker run -v /vol1 --name test ubuntu

$ docker inspect --format='{{.Config.Volumes}}' test
map[/vol1:{}]

$ docker inspect --format='{{.Mounts}}' test
[{volume 563e1ff87f6acc76911713ac15f5edf163d1d2206ef98a57a1dc2de3be44baed
/mnt/sda1/var/lib/docker/volumes/563e1ff87f6acc76911713ac15f5edf163d1d220
6ef98a57a1dc2de3be44baed/_data /vol1 local  true }]

$ docker volume ls
DRIVER              VOLUME NAME
local               563e1ff87f6acc76911713ac15f5edf163d1d2206ef98a57a1dc2
                    de3be44baed

$ docker container ls -a
CONTAINER ID  IMAGE    COMMAND   CREATED         STATUS
  PORTS   NAMES
e13ecdbcddf5  ubuntu   "bash"    2 minutes ago   Exited (0) About a minute ago
        test

$ docker rm -v test
test

$ docker volume ls
DRIVER              VOLUME NAME
```

An alternate way is to define the volume in a Dockerfile. In Listing 5-2, we write a `Dockerfile` to create an image with a volume and build it. Remember to save the file as `Dockerfile` with an uppercase D and without any extensions. Then we craft a container from this image as we did in the previous example using the `docker build` subcommand and `-t` option to name/tag it. Do not forget the `.` at the end of the `docker build` subcommand to indicate that the `Dockerfile` is at the current path and not in a subdirectory.

We repeat the same exact steps as the previous example to verify creating the volume inside the container. The verification will be both using the `docker inspect` subcommand and from the host using the `docker volume ls` subcommand.

Again, to verify that the volume has been created, we use `docker inspect --format= '{{.Config.Volumes}}' <container name or ID>`; the volume name will be displayed. To get the volume ID, we use `docker inspect --format='{{.Mounts}}' <container name or ID>`. All the information of the container volume will be displayed, as well as the paths on the host and inside the container and if its read/write flag equals `true` or not.

From the host, we can get the volumes created by using `docker volume ls`; the volume ID will be displayed in the list. The final step is to remove the container with the volume using `docker rm -v <container name or ID>`. Re-list the volumes using `docker volume ls`; the list will be empty if there are no other containers running.

Listing 5-2. Using the Dockerfile to create a volume inside a container

```
docker@dtr:~$ vi Dockerfile
docker@dtr:~$ cat Dockerfile
FROM ubuntu
VOLUME /vol1
docker@dtr:~$ docker build -t test_image .
Sending build context to Docker daemon  19.46kB
Step 1/2 : FROM ubuntu
 ---> ba6acccedd29
Step 2/2 : VOLUME /vol1
 ---> Running in db907f905682
Removing intermediate container db907f905682
 ---> ba87cee1213b
Successfully built ba87cee1213b
```

```
Successfully tagged test_image:latest
docker@dtr:~$ docker run -it --name test test_image
root@bd277de2e378:/# cd /vol1
root@bd277de2e378:/vol1# exit
exit
docker@dtr:~$ docker inspect --format='{{.Config.Volumes}}' test
map[/vol1:{}]
docker@dtr:~$ docker inspect --format='{{.Mounts}}' test
[{volume ec59f0aa60d1457c48a9046e1d9986c043e154c92ff20abb6d912de217eb7e74
/mnt/sda1/var/lib/docker/volumes/ec59f0aa60d1457c48a9046e1d9986c043e154c9
2ff20abb6d912de217eb7e74/_data /vol1 local  true }]
docker@dtr:~$ docker volume ls
DRIVER              VOLUME NAME
local               ec59f0aa60d1457c48a9046e1d9986c043e154c92ff20abb6d912
                    de217eb7e74
docker@dtr:~$ docker rm -v test
test
docker@dtr:~$ docker volume ls
DRIVER              VOLUME NAME
docker@dtr:~$
```

All the above-mentioned ways to define a volume will mount a persistent one because the sharing is between the container and the Docker host. Therefore, we must be careful when removing the containers with their volumes as well, using the -v option in the docker rm subcommand, unless we are sure that we need the host to keep the data. However, if we forget to do that and find that we are low in space, we can use docker volume prune to remove all the anonymous volumes that were not removed when their containers were removed.

Ephemeral Volumes

This volatile type of storage occurs when sharing a volume between containers. It persists as long as there is at least one container using it. When all the containers using the volume exited, the volume disappears with its data.

To share a volume between containers, we use the `--volumes-from` option in the `docker run` subcommand, as in Listing 5-3. Always think about volumes as shared folders where all the contributors can update and edit their contents. In this scenario, we will create the `first` container with a volume and then create a second container that will share the volume from the `first` using `--volumes-from`. The third step is removing the `first` container with the `-v` option. The container will be removed; however, its volume will remain because the `second` container still uses it. This ephemeral volume persists as long as there is a container using it. The fourth step is checking that volume's presence from inside the `second` container. The fifth step is crafting a `third` container that shares the volume. The sixth step is removing the `second` container with its volume. The seventh step is again checking the volume's presence from inside the `third` container and from the host. The eighth step is to remove this last `third` container with its volume. The final step is checking the volume; we will find that it has gone *poof!* It disappeared because there was no container using it.

Listing 5-3. Creating an ephemeral volume using --volumes-from

```
docker@dtr:~$ docker run -it -v /vol1 --name first ubuntu bash
root@8edef4d9cb32:/# date > /vol1/file1
root@8edef4d9cb32:/# cat /vol1/file1
Sat Mar  5 01:05:53 UTC 2022
root@8edef4d9cb32:/# exit
exit
docker@dtr:~$ docker run -it --volumes-from first --name second ubuntu bash
root@e455ff1b30bb:/# cat /vol1/file1
Thu Jan  6 20:17:13 UTC 2022
root@e455ff1b30bb:/# echo more_data > /vol1/file2
root@e455ff1b30bb:/# cd /vol1
root@e455ff1b30bb:/vol1# ls
file1  file2
root@e455ff1b30bb:/vol1# exit
exit
docker@dtr:~$ docker rm -v first
first
docker@dtr:~$ docker volume ls
```

```
DRIVER                    VOLUME NAME
local                     7666b9af989a706398f813496b287e9479539b8d663f25fb73402
                          21161d96aa7
docker@dtr:~$ docker run -it --volumes-from second --name third ubuntu bash
root@0da0a4d76c41:/# cd /vol1
root@0da0a4d76c41:/vol1# ls
file1   file2
root@0da0a4d76c41:/vol1# exit
exit
docker@dtr:~$ docker rm -v second third
second
third
docker@dtr:~$ docker volume ls
DRIVER              VOLUME NAME
docker@dtr:~$
```

Data-Only Volume

So far, we have shown the ways to define the volume when we create containers. However, in real applications, volumes outlive containers. In this section, we will create volumes outside the containers' scope and learn how to mount them onto containers, as in Listing 5-4.

In Listing 5-4, we start by creating the volume as an independent object using the docker volume create subcommand. To list all the volumes as we did in the previous examples, we use the docker volume ls subcommand. To get the path of that volume at the host, we inspect the volume using the docker volume inspect subcommand.

To mount the volume onto a container, we use the -v <host volume name>:/<container volume name> option in the docker run subcommand. From inside the container, we edit the volume by adding the date in a file inside the container. Then we remove the container with its volume. However, when we check the host volume using docker volume ls, we find that the host volume and its data are still saved. Therefore, this data volume vol outlived the container. To remove this data volume, we use the docker volume rm subcommand. To verify that the volume has been removed, we use the docker volume ls subcommand.

Listing 5-4. Create a data volume

```
docker@dtr:~$ docker volume create vol
vol
docker@dtr:~$ docker volume ls
DRIVER              VOLUME NAME
local               vol
docker@dtr:~$ docker inspect vol
[
    {
        "CreatedAt": "2022-01-06T23:09:41Z",
        "Driver": "local",
        "Labels": {},
        "Mountpoint": "/mnt/sda1/var/lib/docker/volumes/vol/_data",
        "Name": "vol",
        "Options": {},
        "Scope": "local"
    }
]
docker@dtr:~$ docker run -it -v vol:/inside_container --name test
ubuntu bash
root@1aa9c9357f50:/# date > /inside_container/file1
root@1aa9c9357f50:/# cat /inside_container/file1
Thu Jan  6 23:16:24 UTC 2022
root@1aa9c9357f50:/# exit
exit
docker@dtr:~$ docker rm -v test
test
docker@dtr:~$ sudo cat /mnt/sda1/var/lib/docker/volumes/vol/_data/file1
Thu Jan  6 23:16:24 UTC 2022
docker@dtr:~$ docker volume rm vol
vol
docker@dtr:~$ docker volume ls
DRIVER              VOLUME NAME
docker@dtr:~$
```

Filesystem vs. Volume

Confusing data persistence as data on a volume instead of an engraved file in the image is common. Let us have an example to show that in Listings 5-5 and 5-6.

Listing 5-5 saved the date in a file called file1 on the container's volume /vol1. However, after committing the container to an image, file1 and its contents disappeared. Assume that instead of the date, there is crucial information that we want to engrave inside the image before pushing it to the repo. To do that, engrave it as a filesystem inside the container and commit it to an image, as in Listing 5-6.

Listing 5-5. Committing an image after editing a container's volume

```
docker@dtr:~$ docker run -it -v /vol1 --name vol_container ubuntu bash
root@6c372a638dd9:/# date >/vol1/file1
root@6c372a638dd9:/# cd /vol1
root@6c372a638dd9:/vol1# ls
file1
root@6c372a638dd9:/vol1# cat file1
Thu Jan  6 15:57:23 UTC 2022
root@6c372a638dd9:/vol1# exit
exit
docker@dtr:~$ docker commit vol_container vol_image
sha256:a8b3116a15eaba61544f1ae335838497183016edb37b3f206c2e7ae4134c4d02
docker@dtr:~$ docker run -it vol_image
root@e98393f665d0:/# cd /vol1
root@e98393f665d0:/vol1# ls
root@e98393f665d0:/vol1# exit
exit
```

Again, the data in the volume will not be saved after committing the image from the container. Therefore, we must use the filesystem instead to save any crucial data. As in Listing 5-6, instead of using the volume, we create a new directory called new and then save the date in a file called file1 instead of the new directory. After committing the image, when we run a container from this image file_image, we find the file and its contents instead of the directory.

Listing 5-6. Committing an image after editing the container's filesystem

```
docker@dtr:~$ docker run -it --name file_container ubuntu bash
root@6cd663a24b33:/# mkdir new
root@6cd663a24b33:/# cd new
root@6cd663a24b33:/new# date > file1
root@6cd663a24b33:/new# ls
file1
root@6cd663a24b33:/new# cat file1
Thu Jan  6 16:00:07 UTC 2022
root@6cd663a24b33:/new# exit
exit
docker@dtr:~$ docker commit file_container file_image
sha256:c27561595c45d2a6b74c2ca8af5780504b543097f2aa539fda530bb38a10912e
docker@dtr:~$ docker run -it file_image
root@9acf66163a9f:/# cd new
root@9acf66163a9f:/new# ls
file1
root@9acf66163a9f:/new# cat file1
Thu Jan  6 16:00:07 UTC 2022
root@9acf66163a9f:/new# exit
exit
```

Rule of thumb: Never use volumes to store any data during build time and use the filesystem instead to be engraved in the image.

Storage in Kubernetes

The storage in Kubernetes is defined over several phases, as in Figure 5-1. The first one is to have the physical storage connected to the cluster and define its drivers/plugins. The plugin is called the provisioner/Container Storage Interface (CSI), and the provider affords it with the storage disks. The second phase is to make the Kubernetes cluster aware of these storage disks. To do that, you define a persistent volume (PV) YML file. The third phase is using the volumes. The pods or the deployments do that by issuing a ticket to register the volume; we do that by creating a new object called the persistent volume claim (PVC). We create it also by writing a PVC YML file.

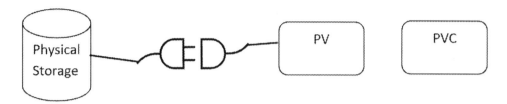

Figure 5-1. *Kubernetes storage*

We can write the YML files as two files, one for the PV and the other for the PVC, or we can write them as one YML file having three dashes in between, as in Listing 5-7.

Listing 5-7. A template sample of a PV and PVC YML file

```
apiVersion: v1
kind: PersistentVolume
metadata:
  name: <PV name>
spec:
  accessModes:
  - ReadWriteOnce
  storageClassName: <sc name>
  capacity:
    storage: <storage size>
  persistentVolumeReclaimPolicy: Retain
  <provisioner parameters>

---
apiVersion: v1
kind: PersistentVolumeClaim
metadata:
  name: <PVC name>
spec:
  accessModes:
  - ReadWriteOnce
  storageClassName: <same sc name as in the PV object>
  resources:
    requests:
      storage: <same storage size as in the PV object>
```

To scale using the storage and having a more robust method, Kubernetes has another object called storage class (SC). Listing 5-8 is an example of the SC template. Storage classes create PVs dynamically. Therefore, we do not need to define the PV individually. It is similar to deployments in Kubernetes that create the pods; it is a similar paradigm.

Listing 5-8. A template sample of the storage class YML file

```
kind: StorageClass
apiVersion: storage.k8s.io/v1
metadata:
        name: <SC name>
<provisioner parameters>
```

Summary

Storage is another crucial concept in Docker and Kubernetes. Storage, networking, and orchestration represent the cornerstone to understand how containers work and Dockerized applications work. Volumes are where all the data is saved. This chapter discussed the persistent and ephemeral types that are within the containers. Moreover, it discussed the data volume as an independent object and not working within the containers. Also, it showed a common error where people save data on persistent volumes within the containers and then commit these containers to images, thinking that the data will be engraved in the new image. However, the volume data is never being uploaded to images. In such cases, such data must be saved in the container filesystem, not the volume, to be engraved in the images. At the end, the chapter discussed Kubernetes storage objects and how to write their manifest files.

CHAPTER 6

Docker Enterprise Edition/Mirantis Kubernetes Engine Installation

In this chapter, you will learn how to install the Docker Enterprise Edition (Docker EE). Since Mirantis acquired Docker, it is rebranding it with the new name of Mirantis Kubernetes Engine (MKE). Installing it is so tricky and has many steps. Normally at a certain step, you will receive an error. Do not panic. You will learn in the chapter how to resolve it and install it correctly.

The Docker EE has three components:

- Docker EE

- UCP (Universal Control Plane)

- DTR (Docker Trusted Registry)

In this chapter, you will learn how to install all of them. Therefore, the chapter will cover the following topics:

- Installing the Docker EE engine. This is an easy step of only two commands.

- Installing the UCP with Kubernetes. This is the tricky part.

- Installing the DTR. Also, this is an easy step.

© Engy Fouda 2022
E. Fouda, *A Complete Guide to Docker for Operations and Development*,
https://doi.org/10.1007/978-1-4842-8117-8_6

Installing the Docker EE on Windows Server 2016

I chose to install the Docker EE on Windows Server 2016 or later because the Docker EE is free to install. For other operating systems, you must buy a plan to install the engine. You can check the Docker documentation for that at `https://docker-docs.netlify. app/install/windows/docker-ee/`.

For installing the Docker EE, you run the following two commands, as in Listing 6-1, in a Windows PowerShell window or a GIT window if you installed GIT.

Listing 6-1. Commands to install the Docker EE on Windows Server 2016 or later

```
Install-Module DockerProvider -Force
Install-Package Docker -ProviderName DockerProvider -Force
```

If the Docker daemon does not start automatically, run the following in PowerShell:
`& 'C:\Program Files\Docker\dockerd.exe'`

Testing the Installation

Let us test the installation to make sure that the Docker engine has been installed correctly. You can do that by running a container, as in Listing 6-2. Figure 6-1 shows the output.

Listing 6-2. Run the hello-world container to verify that you installed the engine correctly

```
$ docker container run hello-world:nanoserver
```

Note   You will not interact directly with the Docker EE. Instead, you'll use the UCP.

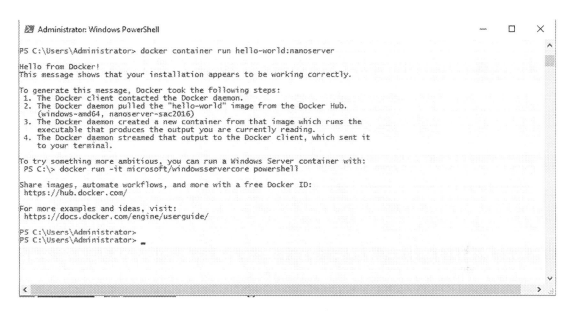

Figure 6-1. *Test the installation*

Installing the UCP

Before you install the UCP, you need to create a couple of nodes in a swarm. Therefore, we need to download Docker Machine to be able to create nodes on the same computer. Download Docker Machine from here: `https://github.com/docker/machine/releases/`. Add the file you download to your folder and rename it as docker-machine. Next, create a cluster on Hyper-V. Create an external virtual switch in the Hyper-V manager. You can create an external switch on Hyper-V following this tutorial: `https://docs.microsoft.com/en-us/windows-server/virtualization/hyper-v/get-started/create-a-virtual-switch-for-hyper-v-virtual-machines`.

In the following section, you will learn how to create some virtual machines (VMs) using Docker Machine step-by-step with screenshots.

Now, we will proceed with the steps to install Kubernetes in UCP. We will start by installing one virtual machine first, where we will create the UCP node, as in step 1, and then will add more later to install the DTR.

Step 1: Create the First Virtual Machine

We must increase the Hyper-V memory to more than 4GB; otherwise, the UCP will not install. If we did not specify the memory size and left the defaults, Docker would generate an error stating that there is not enough memory to install the UCP. To create a VM, run the following command.

Listing 6-3. Create a VM with larger memory than the default and then list the VMs

```
$ docker-machine create -d hyperv --hyperv-virtual-switch "<external switch
name>" --hyperv-memory 15000 <machine name>

$ docker-machine ls
```

In Listing 6-3, we use the `docker-machine create` command to create a VM. To specify the VM's driver, we use the `-d hyperv` option. Then we specify the name of the external switch that we created in a previous step using `--hyperv-virtual-switch "<the external switch name>"`. Then the most crucial one is to increase the memory by adding `--hyperv-memory 15000`. Finally, give the machine a name, for example, `kuber1, myvm1, or trial1`. When you run Listing 6-3, the output will be as in Figure 6-2.

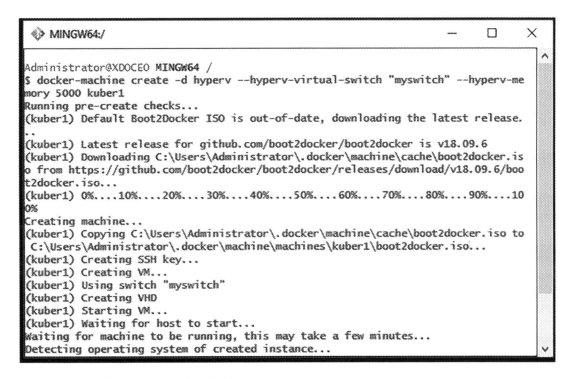

Figure 6-2. *Create your first VM*

The Docker engine will create the machine for you and generate an IP for it. To verify that the machine was created correctly and to get its IP, list all the virtual machines on your cluster, by running `docker-machine ls`.

For further information, check the Docker documentation at `https://docs.docker.com/machine/drivers/hyper-v/`.

If you want to specify a certain IP to the virtual machine and not use the autogenerated one, you can use the `sudo ifconfig` command as in Listing 6-4. Then regenerate the machine certificates using `regenerate-certs`. Finally, re-list the virtual machine to verify the IP that you assigned using `docker-machine ls`.

Listing 6-4. Set a specific IP to your VM

```
$ docker-machine ssh <machine-name> "sudo ifconfig eth0 <IP>"
$ docker-machine regenerate-certs <machine-name>
$ docker-machine ls
```

If it took so long after the ifconfig, click Ctrl+C or Ctrl+X or Ctrl+Z to exit and continue the steps. For more information, you can check the following sites:

https://stackoverflow.com/questions/34336218/is-there-a-way-to-force-docker-machine-to-create-vm-with-a-specific-ip

For VirtualBox, not Hyper-V: https://stackoverflow.com/questions/32639765/how-do-i-create-a-docker-machine-with-a-specific-url-using-docker-machine-and-vi/32649678

Step 2: Initialize a Swarm and Add Nodes

After we created a VM, let us start creating our cluster. We will ssh our VM with docker swarm init to initialize the swarm, as in Listing 6-5.

Listing 6-5. Initialize a swarm

```
$ docker-machine ssh <machine-name> "docker swarm init --advertise-addr
<VM IP>"

$ docker-machine ssh <machine-name> "docker node ls"
```

To specify the VM, we must use its IP address as an entry to the --advertise-addr option. The Docker engine will state that this node is currently the manager, as in Figure 6-3. Also, it will generate a long token to add worker nodes to your swarm. This command we will use later to create another node on another VM and install the DTR on it. Remember that we cannot install the UCP and the DTR on the same node.

```
Administrator@XDOCEO MINGW64 /
$ docker-machine ssh kuber1 "docker swarm init --advertise-addr 172.19.96.209"
Swarm initialized: current node (ush4t89u8p5swzc780wtchlpx) is now a manager.

To add a worker to this swarm, run the following command:

    docker swarm join --token SWMTKN-1-5ivbsgijc7f1caq53d0sellpt5y4hu4xx7u1frrkeug
n6lu6gi-2ivb9ogr93v21mba0ysne2idx 172.19.96.209:2377

To add a manager to this swarm, run 'docker swarm join-token manager' and follow t
he instructions.
```

Figure 6-3. *Initialize a swarm*

To verify that this step was executed correctly, list the nodes that you have in the cluster using the docker node ls command.

To add another node that we will use later to install the Docker Trusted Registry, you create a new virtual machine by running `docker-machine create -d hyperv --hyperv-virtual-switch "<external switch name>" <machine name>`. Note that this time you do not need to increase the memory size, so remove the `--hyperv-memory 15000 <machine name>` option.

To add the second node to the cluster, copy the token that was generated in Figure 6-3 and paste it using `docker-machine ssh <machine name> "docker swarm join –token <token> <machine IP>"`. The Docker daemon will show a message saying that this node was added to the swarm as a worker.

Step 3: Install UCP Version 3.0.0

Now, we have the first node on the first VM. So we are ready to install the UCP. The UCP is merely a container that we will run from an image from `http://hub.docker.com`. Pull the UCP image and run it, as in Listing 6-6. If you did not pull the image first, no problem; the engine will pull it automatically for you before crafting a container from it.

Listing 6-6. Run the UCP container from docker/ucp:3.0.0

```
$ docker-machine ssh <machine-name>

$ docker container run --rm -it --name ucp  -v /var/run/docker.sock:/var/
run/docker.sock docker/ucp:3.0.0 install  --swarm-port 2400 –interactive
```

We will `ssh` to the VM using `docker-machine ssh <machine-name>`. Pull the UCP image, `docker/ucp:3.0.0`, and run it. The `--rm` option is to automatically remove the container when it stops running. The `-it` option is for interactive terminal. The `--name` option is to name the container instead of the autogenerated name that Docker gives as `adjective_noun`. The `-v` option is to specify the volume path at the host and inside the container. Then use the command `install` in the `docker/ucp:3.0.0` image. You can use version 3.0.0 or later. Before that, the UCP was having only a swarm as the orchestrator. Starting from 3.0.0, the Kubernetes was added as another orchestrator in the UCP. Then specify the swarm port as 2400 in the `--swarm-port` option. The `-interactive` option is to be able to enter the values as login name, password, and IP of other nodes in the cluster.

However, a mount error will be generated, as in Figure 6-4. Do not panic; in step 4, we will resolve this mount error. It is easy to resolve.

```
docker@kuber1:~$ docker container run --rm -it --name ucp  -v /var/run/docker.sock
:/var/run/docker.sock   docker/ucp:3.1.5 install  --host-address 172.19.96.209  --
swarm-port 2400 --interactive --san 172.19.96.211
INFO[0000] Your engine version 18.09.6, build 481bc77 (4.14.116-boot2docker) is co
mpatible with UCP 3.1.5 (e3b1ac1)
FATA[0001] Error response from daemon: linux mounts: path /var/lib/kubelet is moun
ted on / but it is not a shared mount Please refer to https://www.docker.com/ddc-4
2 for more information
```

Figure 6-4. *Run the UCP, and an error mount will be generated.*

Step 4: Mount Issue

To resolve this mount error, you need to share some of the folders where Kubernetes will be installed. You can do that by running Listing 6-7. You can read more about this mount issue at https://github.com/kubernetes/kubernetes-anywhere/issues/88.

Listing 6-7. Share the folders

```
$ sudo mount -o bind /var/lib/kubelet /var/lib/kubelet
$ sudo mount --make-shared /var/lib/kubelet
$ sudo mount --make-shared /
```

The output of Listing 6-7 is shown in Figure 6-5.

```
docker@kuber1:~$ sudo mount -o bind /var/lib/kubelet /var/lib/kubelet
docker@kuber1:~$ sudo mount --make-shared /var/lib/kubelet
```

Figure 6-5. *Resolve the mount issue.*

Step 5: Reinstall UCP Version 3.0.0

After resolving the mount issue by sharing the folders, re-craft the container UCP from the docker/ucp:3.0.0 image, as in Listing 6-8. It is the same command that we used in step 3. During installation, enter your username and password when you are prompted to do that.

Listing 6-8. Recreate the UCP container

```
$ docker container run --rm -it --name ucp  -v /var/run/docker.sock:/var/
run/docker.sock   docker/ucp:3.0.0 install  --swarm-port 2400 -interactive
```

The output of Listing 6-8 is shown in Figure 6-6.

```
docker@kuber1:~$ docker container run --rm -it --name ucp  -v /var/run/docker.sock
:/var/run/docker.sock   docker/ucp:3.1.5 install  --host-address 172.19.96.209  --
swarm-port 2400 --interactive --san 172.19.96.211
INFO[0000] Your engine version 18.09.6, build 481bc77 (4.14.116-boot2docker) is co
mpatible with UCP 3.1.5 (e3b1ac1)
Admin Username: admin
Admin Password:
Confirm Admin Password:
INFO[0019] Pulling required images... (this may take a while)
INFO[0019] Pulling docker/ucp-azure-ip-allocator:3.1.5
INFO[0025] Pulling docker/ucp-kube-dns-sidecar:3.1.5
INFO[0029] Pulling docker/ucp-calico-cni:3.1.5
INFO[0038] Pulling docker/ucp-calico-node:3.1.5
```

```
INFO[0011] Pulling docker/ucp-interlock:3.0.0
INFO[0013] Pulling docker/ucp-compose:3.0.0
INFO[0041] Pulling docker/ucp-hyperkube:3.0.0
INFO[0062] Pulling docker/ucp-interlock-extension:3.0.0
INFO[0065] Pulling docker/ucp-interlock-proxy:3.0.0
INFO[0070] Pulling docker/ucp-agent:3.0.0
INFO[0075] Pulling docker/ucp-calico-node:3.0.0
INFO[0088] Pulling docker/ucp-cfssl:3.0.0
INFO[0090] Pulling docker/ucp-etcd:3.0.0
INFO[0096] Pulling docker/ucp-calico-kube-controllers:3.0.0
INFO[0101] Pulling docker/ucp-kube-dns:3.0.0
INFO[0105] Pulling docker/ucp-calico-cni:3.0.0
INFO[0113] Pulling docker/ucp-controller:3.0.0
INFO[0124] Pulling docker/ucp-auth:3.0.0
INFO[0128] Pulling docker/ucp-kube-compose:3.0.0
INFO[0133] Pulling docker/ucp-metrics:3.0.0
INFO[0140] Pulling docker/ucp-pause:3.0.0
INFO[0142] Pulling docker/ucp-swarm:3.0.0
INFO[0146] Pulling docker/ucp-kube-dns-dnsmasq-nanny:3.0.0
INFO[0151] Pulling docker/ucp-kube-dns-sidecar:3.0.0
INFO[0155] Pulling docker/ucp-dsinfo:3.0.0
INFO[0157] Pulling docker/ucp-auth-store:3.0.0
WARN[0164] None of the hostnames we'll be using in the UCP certificates [kuber1 127.0.0.1 172.1
7.0.1] contain a domain component.  Your generated certs may fail TLS validation unless you onl
y use one of these shortnames or IPs to connect.  You can use the --san flag to add more aliase
s
You may enter additional aliases (SANs) now or press enter to proceed with the above list.
Additional aliases:
WARN[0000] Unauthorized users may be able to access this node since it's listening on port 2376
. Learn more at https://docker.com/ddc-18
WARN[0000] Installation will continue in 10 seconds...
INFO[0027] Establishing mutual Cluster Root CA with Swarm
INFO[0030] Installing UCP with host address 172.19.96.225 - If this is incorrect, please specif
y an alternative address with the '--host-address' flag
INFO[0030] Generating UCP Client Root CA
INFO[0030] Deploying UCP Service
INFO[0237] Installation completed on kuber1 (node stycjb4pgvpr2rxx1d74y67dz)
INFO[0237] UCP Instance ID: yzuwboiew27aho244t6tvszz4
INFO[0237] UCP Server SSL: SHA-256 Fingerprint=A5:81:1F:AA:E9:7B:10:EC:A1:09:6D:E7:63:1A:4C:25:
E6:D5:8F:18:28:63:AF:A8:85:B7:CC:F4:DF:6A:ED:26
INFO[0237] Login to UCP at https://172.19.96.225:443
INFO[0237] Username: admin
INFO[0237] Password: (your admin password)
docker@kuber1:~$
```

Figure 6-6. *Installing UCP*

Congratulations! You installed the UCP correctly. You can access it from the browser
by entering http://<UCP node IP>/443. You can reach the UCP interface/service through
port 443 of the UCP container. Enter your username and password. You will be asked to

upload the license or skip. You can skip it, but after logging in, you will not find all the features enabled. Therefore, follow along to step 6.

Step 6: Upload the License

Before Mirantis acquired Docker, you could have downloaded a 30-day license to try out the Docker EE for free. Now, there is not this option anymore up till writing this book. Maybe soon, Mirantis will change its marketing plans and return this option. For the time being, you can download my license and use it from `http://engyfoda.com/` `docker_subscription.lic`.

Step 7: Install Kubernetes CLI

Now, you are good to go to start using the graphical user interface (GUI). However, the best practice is to install the Kubernetes client (CLI) to be able to write the Kubernetes command at the shell. To install the Kubernetes CLI, on the left menu, click admin ➤ My Profile ➤ New Client Bundle, as shown in Figure 6-7. A ZIP file will be downloaded to your Windows Downloads folder.

Figure 6-7. *Generate a new client bundle*

To transfer this ZIP file from your local Windows machine to the VM, you need to use the SCP command, as in Listing 6-9. You will be asked to enter a password. Always enter `tcuser`.

A message will state that the file has been transferred. To verify that, log in to your VM using SSH and use the `ls` command to list all the files that are on your VM. The ZIP is listed. Now unzip it with the `unzip` command and run the shell file saved in the ZIP file as `env.sh`.

Listing 6-9. Use the SCP to transfer the ZIP file from Windows to the VM

```
cd Downloads/
docker-machine scp ucp-bundle-admin.zip <VM name>:~
docker-machine ssh <VM name>
ls
unzip ucp-bundle-admin.zip
eval "$(<env.sh)"
```

If there are no errors, you are good to go to step 8. However, if the SCP generated an error, as in Figure 6-8, you need to regenerate the key for the VM using ssh-keygen -R <VM IP>, as in Listing 6-10. Rerun the previous step again starting from the SCP command and enter the password as tcuser. Finally, unzip the file.

```
Administrator@XDOCEO MINGW64 /
$ docker-machine scp myvm1:~/ucp.bkp firstapp/
cp: cannot stat 'Files\Git\usr\bin\scp.exe': No such file or directory
cp: cannot stat 'C:\Program': No such file or directory
cp: cannot stat 'Files\Git\usr\bin\scp.exe': No such file or directory
cp: cannot stat '-o': No such file or directory
cp: cannot stat 'StrictHostKeyChecking=no': No such file or directory
cp: cannot stat '-o': No such file or directory
cp: cannot stat 'UserKnownHostsFile=/dev/null': No such file or directory
cp: cannot stat '-o': No such file or directory
cp: cannot stat 'LogLevel=quiet': No such file or directory
cp: cannot stat '-3': No such file or directory
cp: cannot stat '-o': No such file or directory
cp: cannot stat 'IdentitiesOnly=yes': No such file or directory
cp: cannot stat '-o': No such file or directory
cp: cannot stat 'Port=22': No such file or directory
cp: cannot stat '-o': No such file or directory
ssh: Could not resolve hostname identityfile=c: Name or service not known
@@@@@@@@@@@@@@@@@@@@@@@@@@@@@@@@@@@@@@@@@@@@@@@@@@@@@@@@@@@@@@@@@@@
@    WARNING: REMOTE HOST IDENTIFICATION HAS CHANGED!    @
@@@@@@@@@@@@@@@@@@@@@@@@@@@@@@@@@@@@@@@@@@@@@@@@@@@@@@@@@@@@@@@@@@@
IT IS POSSIBLE THAT SOMEONE IS DOING SOMETHING NASTY!
Someone could be eavesdropping on you right now (man-in-the-middle attack)!
It is also possible that a host key has just been changed.
The fingerprint for the ECDSA key sent by the remote host is
SHA256:3w1u1/6ODOroUGpyHyGYBR92ZPYbabM/Y3+O7CS6N8s.
Please contact your system administrator.
Add correct host key in /c/Users/Administrator/.ssh/known_hosts to get rid of th
is message.
Offending ECDSA key in /c/Users/Administrator/.ssh/known_hosts:7
ECDSA host key for 172.19.96.207 has changed and you have requested strict check
ing.
Host key verification failed.
exit status 1
```

Figure 6-8. *The SCP error*

You can get the manager IP by running the docker-machine ls command. It will list the nodes with their IP addresses.

Listing 6-10. Resolve the SCP error

```
$ ssh-keygen -R <manager IP>
docker-machine scp ucp-bundle-admin.zip <VM name>:~
docker-machine ssh <VM name>
ls
unzip ucp-bundle-admin.zip
eval "$(<env.sh)"
```

Step 8: Install the kubectl Binary via curl

After you installed the Kubernetes CLI, install the kubectl binary using the curl command, as in Listing 6-11. For more information, you can check the documentation at https:// v1-11.docs.kubernetes.io/docs/tasks/tools/install-kubectl/. In Listing 6-11, there are two curl commands pointing to two sites. You can use one of them to install kubectl.

Listing 6-11. Install the kubectl binary via curl

```
$ curl -LO https://storage.googleapis.com/kubernetes-release/release/$
(curl -s https://storage.googleapis.com/kubernetes-release/release/stable.
txt)/bin/linux/amd64/kubectl
```

```
$ curl -LO https://storage.googleapis.com/kubernetes-release/release/
v1.8.3/bin/linux/amd64/kubectl
```

```
$ chmod +x ./kubectl
$ sudo mv ./kubectl /usr/local/bin/kubectl
$ kubectl cluster-info
```

After you run the curl command, run the chmod command, as in Listing 6-11. Then move the binary to the folder /usr/local/bin/kubectl. Finally, verify that the kubectl was installed correctly by getting the cluster info, as shown in Figure 6-9. If you received both addresses for the Kubernetes master and KubeDNS, your installation is correct.

```
docker@kuber1:~$ curl -LO https://storage.googleapis.com/kubernetes-release/rele
ase/$(curl -s https://storage.googleapis.com/kubernetes-release/release/stable.t
xt)/bin/linux/amd64/kubectl
  % Total    % Received % Xferd  Average Speed   Time    Time     Time  Current
                                 Dload  Upload   Total   Spent    Left  Speed
100 41.1M  100 41.1M    0     0  6678k      0  0:00:06  0:00:06 --:--:-- 6184k
docker@kuber1:~$ chmod +x ./kubectl
docker@kuber1:~$ sudo mv ./kubectl /usr/local/bin/kubectl
docker@kuber1:~$ kubectl cluster-info
Kubernetes master is running at https://172.19.96.214:6443
KubeDNS is running at https://172.19.96.214:6443/api/v1/namespaces/kube-system/s
ervices/kube-dns:dns/proxy

To further debug and diagnose cluster problems, use 'kubectl cluster-info dump'.
```

Figure 6-9. *Install the kubectl binary via curl*

If not and you received only for the Kubernetes master and no KubeDNS was displayed, rerun the steps of Listing 6-11 starting from trying the other curl path.

Verify that you installed kubectl correctly by running two kubectl commands to get its version and get the help, as in Listing 6-12.

Listing 6-12. Verify the kubectl installation

```
$ kubectl version
$ kubectl --help
```

The output of Listing 6-12 is shown in Figure 6-10.

```
docker@kuber1:~$ kubectl version
Client Version: version.Info{Major:"1", Minor:"14", GitVersion:"v1.14.2", GitCom
mit:"66049e3b21efe110454d67df4fa62b08ea79a19b", GitTreeState:"clean", BuildDate:
"2019-05-16T16:23:09Z", GoVersion:"go1.12.5", Compiler:"gc", Platform:"linux/amd
64"}
Server Version: version.Info{Major:"1", Minor:"11+", GitVersion:"v1.11.8-docker-
1", GitCommit:"b7a0d533758a3a4dda2a8aa632f88eafc589da90", GitTreeState:"clean",
BuildDate:"2019-03-01T22:07:27Z", GoVersion:"go1.10.8", Compiler:"gc", Platform:
"linux/amd64"}
docker@kuber1:~$ kubectl --help
kubectl controls the Kubernetes cluster manager.

 Find more information at:
https://kubernetes.io/docs/reference/kubectl/overview/

Basic Commands (Beginner):
  create         Create a resource from a file or from stdin.
  expose         Take a replication controller, service, deployment or pod and
expose it as a new Kubernetes Service
  run            Run a particular image on the cluster
  set            Set specific features on objects

Basic Commands (Intermediate):
  explain        Documentation of resources
  get            Display one or many resources
  edit           Edit a resource on the server
  delete         Delete resources by filenames, stdin, resources and names, or
by resources and label selector
```

Figure 6-10. *Verify that you installed kubectl correctly*

Installing the DTR

As we mentioned before, we cannot install the DTR on the same node as the
UCP. Therefore, your swarm must have more than one node to be able to install the UCP
and DTR. To create another node as a worker in our swarm, you must run the command
that was generated for you when you initialized the swarm, as in Figure 6-3, that we
mentioned before. You run at the shell.

After having another node, go to UCP web UI ➤ admin ➤ Admin Settings ➤
DTR. Write the IP of the second node in the DTR external URL. Choose the second node
in UCP node. Check PEM-CA. Then copy the generated code. It should look like this:

```
docker run -it --rm docker/dtr install  --dtr-external-
url 172.19.96.242  --ucp-username admin  --ucp-url
https://172.19.96.245  --ucp-ca "-----BEGIN CERTIFICATE-----
```

```
MIIBgDCCASegAwIBAgIUUl8U5EBlbgYqM21rJtiMBQlL2IswCgYIKoZIzjOEAwIw
HTEbMBkGA1UEAxMSVUNQIENsaWVudCBSb29OIENBMB4XDTE4MTIyMDAyMDMwMFoX
DTIzMTIxOTAyMDMwMFowHTEbMBkGA1UEAxMSVUNQIENsaWVudCBSb290IENBMFkw
EwYHKoZIzjOCAQYIKoZIzjODAQcDQgAEmWoEwBONKbFOkaHTJCkmP/D15uJBnCYN
2ArYZGfvhOKwP9kWUsGXkjNPuc1Wik4M+/GVLYeqYPepQUO8RoeOxqNFMEMwDgYD
VROPAQH/BAQDAgEGMBIGA1UdEwEB/wQIMAYBAf8CAQIwHQYDVROOBBYEFJaNEWv6
gqTsvIWHsansdoxeZZJtMAoGCCqGSM49BAMCAOcAMEQCIGdkztU1MNNDVl3hxELw
vlK5zo4WBpcGAnFDWOjz9toTAiAIFLTOLsfefOv/Cj5ha787FLG9ifefJH4IP7iM
YQepkg==
-----END CERTIFICATE-----
"
```

Go to the shell and SSH to the second node using `docker-machine ssh <second node for DTR>` and paste the generated code from the previous step, which has the certificate encoding. This command runs a container from the DTR image, `docker/dtr`. The rest of the command has the choices when we made the UCP web interface. The DTR should be installed with TLS for the <second node URL>, as shown in Figure 6-11.

```
INFO[0045] Waiting for database dtr2 to exist
INFO[0046] Establishing connection with Rethinkdb
INFO[0046] Generated TLS certificate.              dnsNames="[]" domains="[172.19
.96.242]" ipAddresses="[172.19.96.242]"
INFO[0047] License config not copied from UCP because UCP has no valid license.
INFO[0047] Migrating db...
INFO[0000] Establishing connection with Rethinkdb
INFO[0000] Migrating database schema               fromVersion=0 toVersion=10
INFO[0007] Waiting for database notaryserver to exist
INFO[0010] Waiting for database notarysigner to exist
INFO[0011] Waiting for database jobrunner to exist
INFO[0015] Migrated database from version 0 to 10
INFO[0062] Starting all containers...
INFO[0062] Getting container configuration and starting containers...
INFO[0062] Automatically configuring rethinkdb cache size to 2000 mb
INFO[0063] Recreating dtr-rethinkdb-3a0fc4debc1b...
INFO[0070] Creating dtr-registry-3a0fc4debc1b...
INFO[0107] Creating dtr-garant-3a0fc4debc1b...
INFO[0130] Creating dtr-api-3a0fc4debc1b...
INFO[0158] Creating dtr-notary-server-3a0fc4debc1b...
INFO[0183] Recreating dtr-nginx-3a0fc4debc1b...
INFO[0215] Creating dtr-jobrunner-3a0fc4debc1b...
INFO[0532] Creating dtr-notary-signer-3a0fc4debc1b...
```

Figure 6-11. *Install the DTR*

Verify Logging from CLI from Both Nodes

After installing the DTR successfully, we need to make sure that we can log in to both nodes of the UCP and the DTR using the username and password that were created in step 5. Use Docker login $docker login <DTR IP>. Enter username, password. It should give login succeeded as shown in Figure 6-12.

Then verify that you can log in to the UCP node by opening a new shell window and using docker login <UCP IP>. Enter username, password. It should give login succeeded as shown in Figure 6-12.

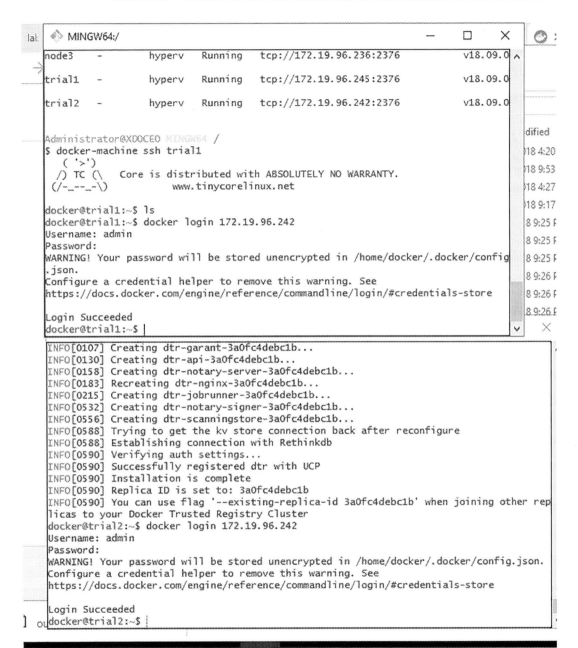

Figure 6-12. *Verify logging from CLI from both nodes*

Verify DTR Installation from UCP Web UI

We need to verify from the UCP web UI that the DTR was installed correctly as well. You can do that by going to the browser where you opened the UCP. Click on the left menu Admin Settings ➤ DTR. You should find the DTR IP and not the menus anymore, as in Figure 6-13, indicating that the DTR is installed at that URL. Copy the URL. Now open a new tab in your browser and paste it.

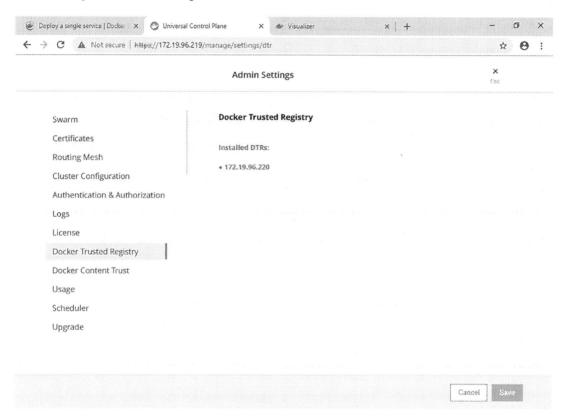

Figure 6-13. *Verify DTR installation from the UCP Web UI*

In that new tab, the DTR should open and look as in Figure 6-14.

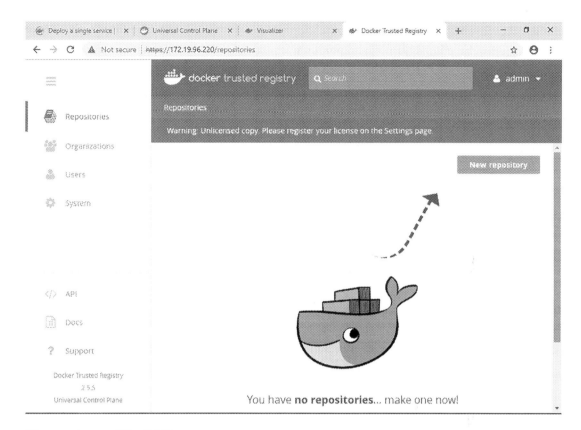

Figure 6-14. *The DTR*

Summary

The chapter covered Docker EE, UCP, and DTR installations on Windows Server and Hyper-V. The DCA does not include questions about these steps. However, you cannot proceed with the upcoming chapters without having the three components up and running. So far, I did not find a book that covers the installation steps and how to resolve the errors that are being generated, which are not in the Docker documentation either. I learned this chapter's content and these steps the hard way. Therefore, I decided to document them in this chapter to save the readers the hassle I faced.

CHAPTER 7

Universal Control Plane (UCP)

In the previous chapter, we learned how to install the Docker Enterprise Edition (Docker EE) and the Universal Control Plane (UCP) user interface (UI). Consequently, in this chapter, we will learn the UCP, the interface of the Enterprise Edition. When you install the Docker Enterprise Edition, you have to either use the command line as you do in the Docker Community Edition or use mouse clicks instead. There is no specific section in the exam about the interface. However, it is crucial to understand the different interfaces according to the UCP versions.

Therefore, the chapter will cover the following topics:

- The interface
- The different UCP versions
- Switching between orchestrators
- Docker Content Trust

© Engy Fouda 2022
E. Fouda, *A Complete Guide to Docker for Operations and Development*,
https://doi.org/10.1007/978-1-4842-8117-8_7

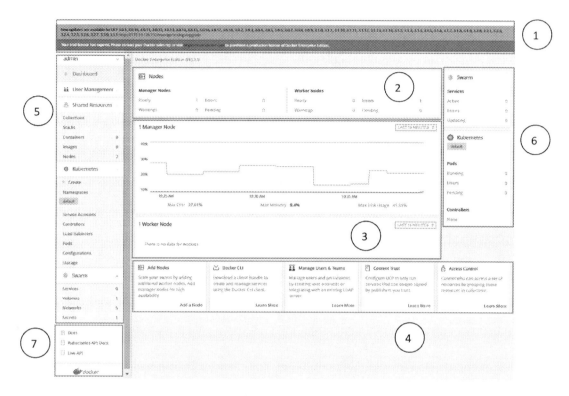

Figure 7-1. *UCP user interface (UI)*

The Interface

The UCP interface, as shown in Figure 7-1, is divided into seven sections. ① At the top of the UCP UI, any notifications, updates, and warnings about the service are displayed.

The interface is divided into two or more panels depending on the UCP version. In all interfaces, the middle pane is standard. Therefore, we shall start with it first.

② In this section, the Docker daemon displays a quick summary of the status of the nodes – how many managers and worker nodes are in the cluster and if they are ready or having errors or pending. Also, it displays any node warnings.

③ In the middle section of this panel, the Docker daemon shows the CPU, memory, and disk space usage in real time for your nodes.

④ This section acts as shortcuts for adding a node and installing the Docker client (CLI) to use the command prompt and not rely on the UI only. Also, the shortcuts include managing the users and teams and integrating the LDAP to import

your company's users and teams, to export the environment variable DOCKER_
CONTENT_TRUST=1 to sign the images, as we will discuss later in Chapter 11. The
last option is a shortcut for the Role-Based Access Control (RBAC), which we will
discuss in Chapter 11.

⑤ ⑥ We will learn more about these panels, 5 and 6, in more detail in the next section
because they change according to the UCP version.

⑦ This last panel has shortcuts for the documentation for Docker, Kubernetes, and
the API.

Different UCP Versions

The UCP has plenty of versions. You can check all the release notes for every version
at this link: `https://docker-docs.netlify.app/ee/ucp/release-notes/`. The UCP
interface before version 3 looks like Figure 7-2.

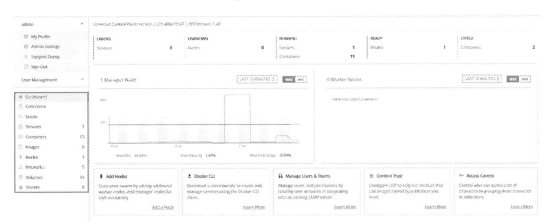

Figure 7-2. *UCP version 2.2.9*

The main difference between this version and version 3.x.x is mainly the left
panel that displays the orchestrators and the resources. Figure 7-2 does not show any
orchestrators. Up till version 2.2.9, only the swarm as the orchestrator came out of the
box. Starting from UCP version 3.3.0, the Kubernetes has been added to the default
orchestrators, as shown in Figure 7-3.

Figure 7-3. *UCP version 3.0.0*

Moreover, Figure 7-3 shows that a right panel has always been added to offer the swarm services and the Kubernetes pods and controllers' statuses.

The shared resources between the two orchestrators are collections, stacks, containers, images, and nodes. For the Kubernetes objects, there are namespaces, service accounts, controllers, load balancers, pods, configurations, and storage. Furthermore, the swarm objects are services, volumes, networks, and secrets. This structure is more organizational than being entirely isolated because the Docker EE gives the option to switch automatically between orchestrators, which we shall see later in the chapter.

Moreover, if you create a secret in the swarm, you can still access it using Kubernetes.

Switching Between Orchestrators

Switching between swarm and Kuberetentes can be done automatically using the UI, which is an excellent feature. To do that, on the left panel, expand the "admin" menu and click Admin Settings, as in Figure 7-4.

admin
My Profile
Admin Settings
Support Dump
About Docker EE
Sign Out
Nodes
Manager Nodes
Worker Nodes
Swarm
Services

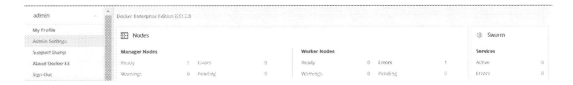

Figure 7-4. *Admin Settings*

Inside Admin Settings, there are plenty of options, and we have already used the license. In the next section, we show how to set Docker Content Trust. Also, we discuss the Docker Trusted Registry in detail in the next chapter. In this section, we focus on switching the new node orchestrator between swarm and Kubernetes. As in Figure 7-5, click Scheduler in the Admin Settings menu.

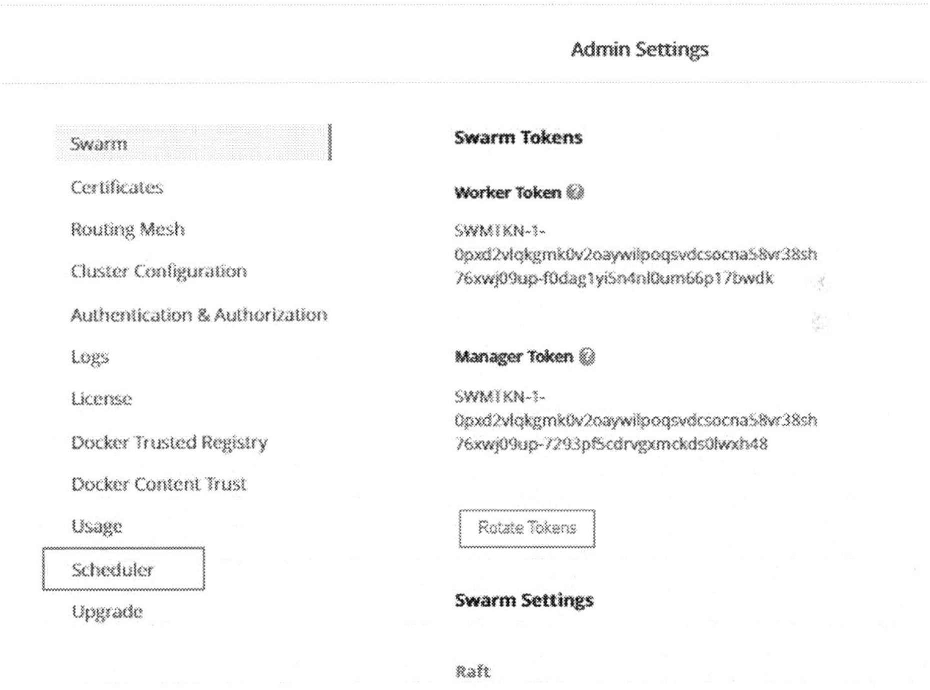

Admin Settings
Swarm
Certificates
Routing Mesh
Cluster Configuration
Authentication & Authorization
Logs
License
Docker Trusted Registry
Docker Content Trust
Usage
Scheduler
Upgrade
Swarm Tokens
Worker Token
SWMTKN-1-
0pxd2vlqkgmk0v2oaywilpoqsvdcsocna58vr38sh
76xwj09up-f0dag1yi5n4nl0um66p17bwdk
Manager Token
SWMTKN-1-
0pxd2vlqkgmk0v2oaywilpoqsvdcsocna58vr38sh
76xwj09up-7293pf5cdrvgxmckds0lwxh48
Rotate Tokens
Swarm Settings
Raft

Figure 7-5. *Scheduler*

Figure 7-6 shows how easy to set the orchestrator type for the new node and switch between them. Do not forget to click Save at the bottom.

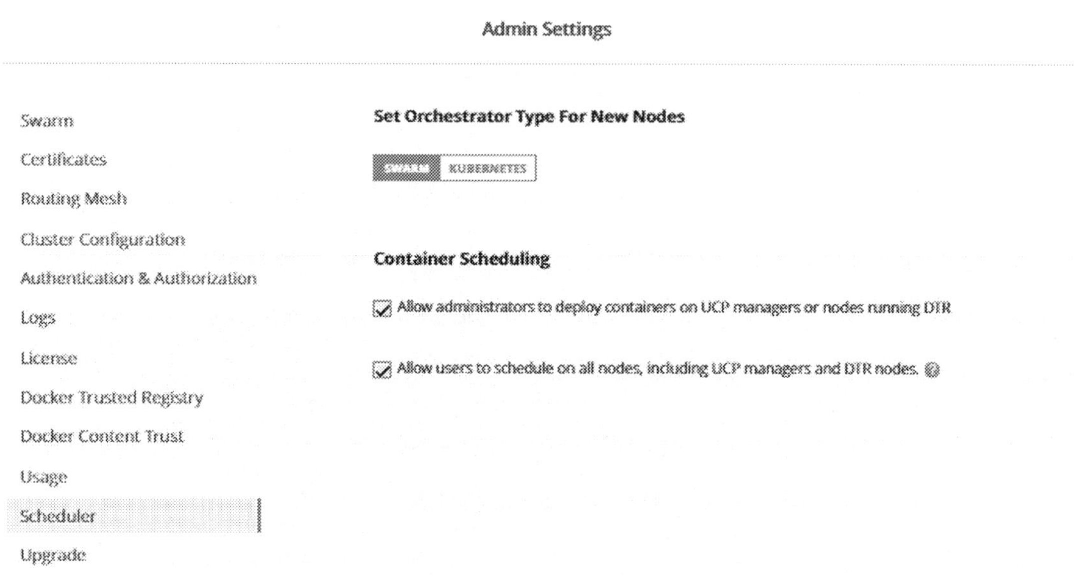

Admin Settings

Swarm

Certificates

Routing Mesh

Cluster Configuration

Authentication & Authorization

Logs

License

Docker Trusted Registry

Docker Content Trust

Usage

Scheduler

Upgrade

Set Orchestrator Type For New Nodes

SWARM   KUBERNETES

Container Scheduling

☑ Allow administrators to deploy containers on UCP managers or nodes running DTR

☑ Allow users to schedule on all nodes, including UCP managers and DTR nodes. ⊘

Figure 7-6. *Select your orchestrator*

Docker Content Trust

Security is crucial, and Docker Content Trust (DCT) is one of the security features in Docker and Kubernetes. We will discuss its function and how to do it using the command prompt in Chapter 11. Therefore, we briefly show how to export this environment variable using the UCP UI. You need to check the box of Run only signed images, as in Figure 7-7. After you save that, the Docker daemon will run only signed images. Moreover, you can specify this feature for a particular team or organization, as shown in the options in Figure 7-7.

Admin Settings   ×
                                                                          Exit

Swarm   **Content Trust Settings**

Certificates   ☑ Run only signed images ⚙

Routing Mesh

Cluster Configuration   Select an Org and then Team in that Org. Signatures from all Teams listed required.
                                   Add Team +
Authentication & Authorization
                                   Any UCP user can sign
Logs

License

Docker Trusted Registry

• *Docker Content Trust*

Usage

Scheduler

Upgrade

                                                                   Cancel   Save

Figure 7-7. *Docker Content Trust (DCT)*

Summary

In conclusion, the Docker UCP UI has plenty of features that we explore in this book.
In this book, we will discuss only the features that are related to the DCA exam.
However, there are more that are beyond the book's scope. Therefore, please explore
and play around with the menus and the options. The UCP provides descriptions and
documentation at every choice, menu, and page, which is helpful and saves you so
much time digging in the documentation. The interface is friendly and easier to use than
memorizing all the Docker commands. However, for the DCA exam, you must learn the
commands and be familiar with the interface.

CHAPTER 8

Docker Trusted Registry (DTR)

In the previous chapter, we learned how to use the UCP UI. Consequently, in this chapter, we will learn the Docker Trusted Registry (DTR). When you install the UCP, you have access to install the DTR from the Admin Settings of the UCP. The questions about this chapter are usually included within the security section of the exam.

Therefore, the chapter will cover the following topics:

- Installing the DTR from the UCP

- Enabling/disabling image scanning

- Pushing an image to the DTR repository

- Immutable images

- Image pruning

Install the DTR from the UCP

To install the DTR, you must have at least two nodes in your cluster. We already installed the UCP on one node and will install the DTR on the other. If you installed both on the same node, the Docker daemon will not object or generate errors. However, you will never be able to have access to the DTR as it uses the same port 443 as the UCP. Hence, when you try to access, the UCP will be displayed.

© Engy Fouda 2022
E. Fouda, *A Complete Guide to Docker for Operations and Development*,
https://doi.org/10.1007/978-1-4842-8117-8_8

Figure 8-1 shows how to install the DTR:

1. On the left menu, click admin ➤ Admin Settings ➤ Docker Trusted Registry.

2. Write the IP of the second node in the DTR external URL.

3. Choose the second node in UCP node.

4. Select PEM-CA.

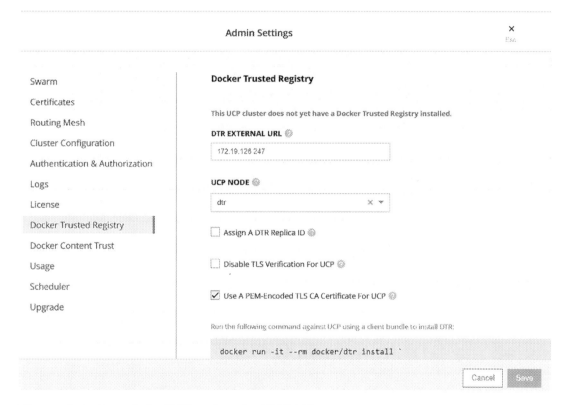

Figure 8-1. *Install the DTR using the UCP UI*

5. Copy the generated code. It should look like Figure 8-2.

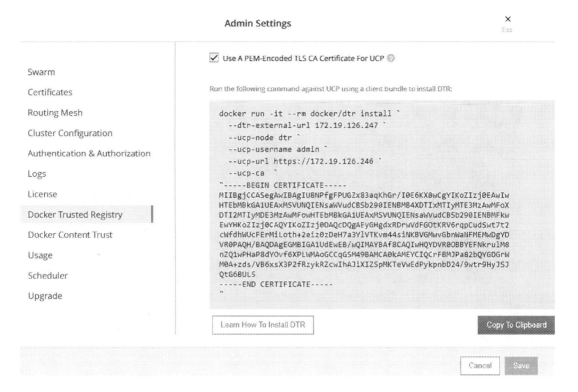

Figure 8-2. *Copy the generated code to the clipboard*

6. docker-machine ssh <second node for DTR>

7. Then paste the generated code.

8. The DTR should be installed with TLS for the <second node URL>.
    It should like Figure 8-3.

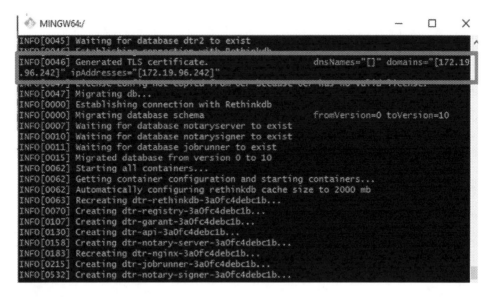

Figure 8-3. *TLS certificate*

When the DTR is successfully installed, go again to admin ➤
Admin Settings ➤ Docker Trusted Registry. It will display the IP
address of the second node, as in Figure 8-4. Copy and paste in the
browser. The DTR IP will be displayed. You will not find the DTR
installation options anymore.

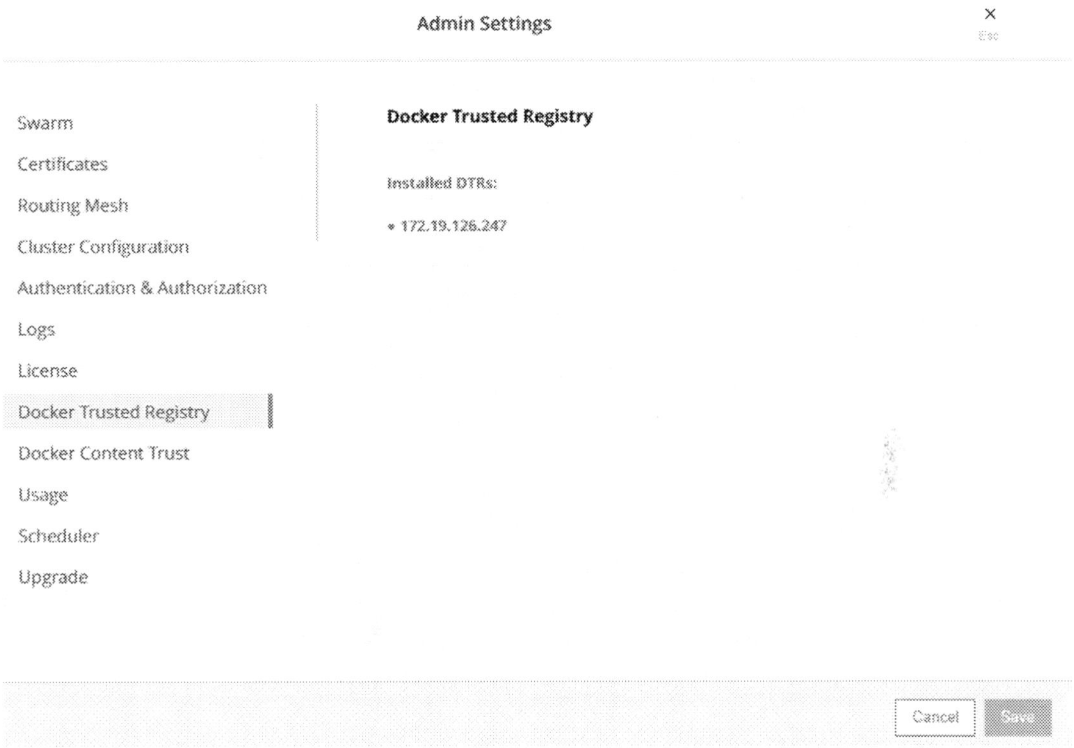

Admin Settings   ✕
                                                        Esc

Swarm   **Docker Trusted Registry**

Certificates
                               Installed DTRs:
Routing Mesh
                               • 172.19.126.247
Cluster Configuration

Authentication & Authorization

Logs

License

Docker Trusted Registry

Docker Content Trust

Usage

Scheduler

Upgrade

                                                   Cancel   Save

Figure 8-4. *The DTR IP address*

You can verify installing the DTR using the CLI by logging from it from both nodes:

1. Type docker login <DTR IP>.

2. Enter username, password.

3. It should give login succeeded. Figure 8-5 is an example for that.
    In this example, the two nodes are called trial1 and trial2, where
    the UCP is installed on trial1 and the DTR is installed on trial2.

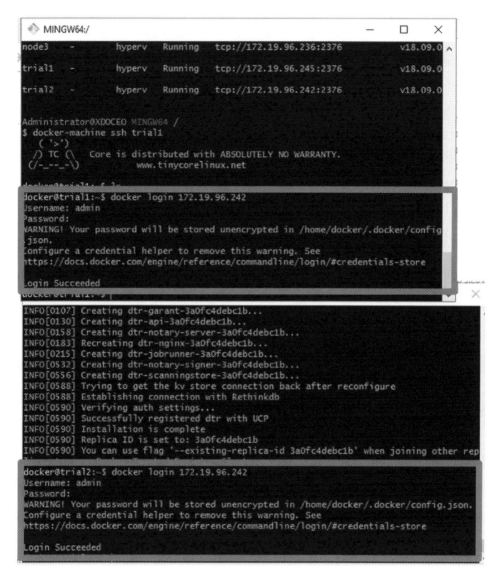

Figure 8-5. *Verify logging from the UCP and DTR from the CLI*

Enable/Disable Image Scanning

In the DTR, enabling and disabling image scanning is easily done by clicking on the left menu System ➤ Security tab ➤ Enable Scanning, as in Figure 8-6.

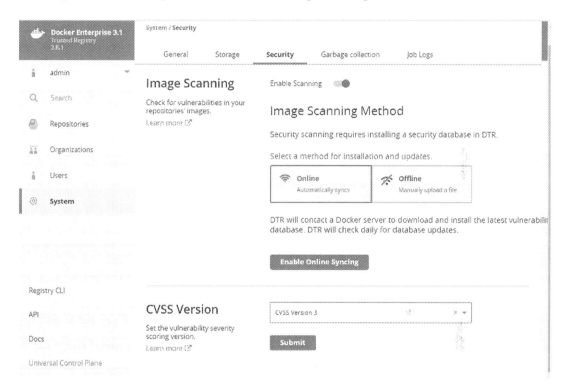

Figure 8-6. *Image scanning*

Push an Image to the DTR Repository

The organization and team changes that you have made in the UCP will be reflected in the DTR and vice versa because they share the same user database. In this example, we will use the admin user and will not create a new user in this chapter. We will learn how to create organizations, teams, and users later in Chapter 11.

To try pushing an image to the DTR, as in Listing 8-1, you can first pull an image using docker pull <image name> and re-tag it to have the DTR URL or IP address using docker tag <image name> <IP/user/image name>. Log in to the DTR using the CLI using docker login <DTR IP address>. The final step is to push the image using docker push <IP/user/image name>.

101

Listing 8-1. Push an image to the DTR

```
docker pull busybox
docker tag busybox 172.19.126.247/admin/firstimage
docker login 172.19.126.247
docker push 172.19.126.247/admin/firstimage
```

Verify that the image has been submitted correctly by clicking on the left menu Repositories ➤ Tags or Images.

The tabs differ depending on the DTR version. Some versions have it under Tags, and older versions show this data under the Images tab.

Immutable Images

Setting the image as immutable is to prevent it from being overwritten and deleted. This option is usually selected for any image after being scanned and promoted. If any user tried to delete this image, an error would be generated. To set the immutability on, select from the left menu Repositories ➤ Settings ➤ Immutability tab, as in Figure 8-7.

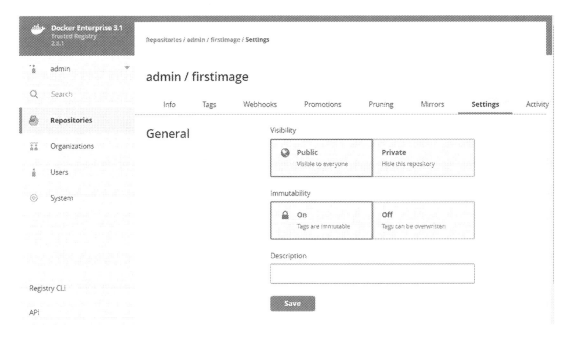

Figure 8-7. *Immutable images*

Image Pruning

Pruning removes the unused images automatically by setting the pruning policies. To do that, select from the left menu Repositories ➤ Pruning tab, as in Figure 8-8.

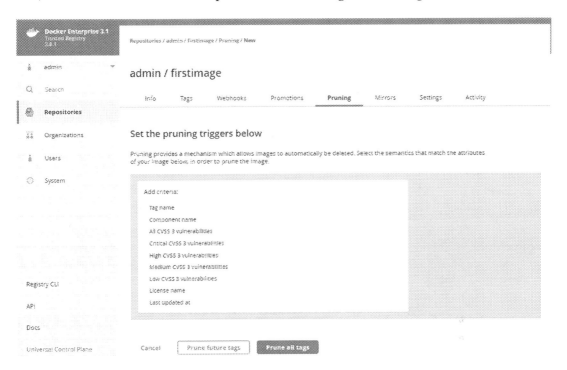

Figure 8-8. *Pruning policies*

Summary

The Docker Trusted Registry is the registry that comes out of the box with the Docker EE. There are plenty of other registries in the market. However, the DCA asks about the DTR interface and options. It is user-friendly and easy to use. Some of its options are discussed in this chapter, for example, how to enable image scanning, how to push images after scanning, immutable images, and image pruning. There are much more options that are available. Please feel free to explore them and learn more about them from the Docker documentation.

CHAPTER 9

Microservices

In this chapter, we will learn about how Docker is boosting the microservices architecture vs. the monolithic one. We will discuss the road map of containerizing an app and how to switch from monolithic to microservices. This road map is generic, regardless of the programming language used. To demonstrate that, we will have three examples for three different programming languages.

Therefore, the chapter will cover the following topics:

- Microservices vs. monolithic

- Process of containerizing an app

- Python example

- Java example

- Visual Studio links

Microservices vs. Monolithic

Monolithic applications usually consist of three components: client-side code, server-side code, and database(s), as in Figure 9-1. Some systems use the data access object (DAO) as an abstract interface to the database. Therefore, when any edit is needed, even a simple one as changing a font color on one of the application pages, the developers have to stop the service for maintenance, edit the code, recompile the whole application, and relaunch.

© Engy Fouda 2022
E. Fouda, *A Complete Guide to Docker for Operations and Development*,
https://doi.org/10.1007/978-1-4842-8117-8_9

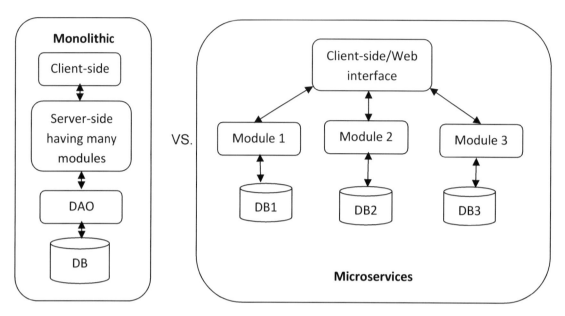

Figure 9-1. *Monolithic vs. microservices*

On the other hand, microservices applications are more robust and agile. As its name implies, it relies on dividing the application into small services. Editing these services does not require to halt the application and can be done on the fly to achieve zero downtime. Moreover, the service can be used in multiple applications at the same time. The database is not central but divided according to the application's tables.

Let us have an example to demonstrate the difference between both architectures. Assume that we want to design a human resources system. The monolithic would be having all the code intercorrelated as in Figure 9-2, and editing is so complicated. On the other hand, in the microservices, every module is independent and lighter, and every service can be edited independently from the rest of the application.

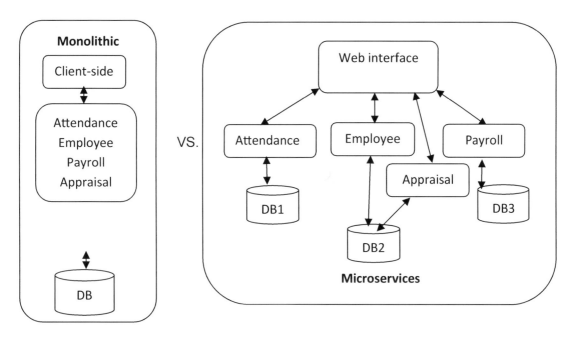

Figure 9-2. *Human resources system in monolithic vs. microservices*

Process of Containerizing an App

Switching from monolithic to microservices is challenging; however, it is highly required to update the outdated system and to be able to deploy it using Docker. The advantage of using Docker is that you encapsulate the service with its dependencies, ship it as an image to a repo, and deploy it. The first step is analyzing your application's code to find the modules and their dependencies and requirements. The second step is dividing the module code independently and writing a Dockerfile for every service to run correctly. The third step is to feed the Dockerfile into the `docker image build` command. The fourth step is to write a YML file for your orchestrator if you have more than one service in your application. The fifth step is to push your images to the repository. The final step is to deploy the app as a container or, if there are many replicas of the container, then run it as a service and, if you have more than one service, then deploy as a stack.

Recap to the containerization of your legacy application:

1. Start with the application code and analyze it.

2. Create a Dockerfile that describes the app, its dependencies, and how to run it.

3. Feed the Dockerfile into the docker image build command.

4. If it is one container, no need to write a YML file. However, if there are more than one service, where each has a folder and a Dockerfile, we should write a YML file to orchestrate between them.

5. Push the image(s) to the registry.

6. Deploy the app as a container/service/stack.

In the coming sections, we will start practicing gradually the previous steps using different languages to prove that the language does not matter in containerization.

Python Example

In this example, assume we have a simple Python program converting from kilograms to pounds, as in Listing 9-1, and we want to convert this app to a web app and containerize it.

Listing 9-1. Kg to pounds Python converter

```
kg=int(input())
print(pound_converter(kg))
def pound_converter(kg):
    pounds = float(kg) * 2.2
    pounds = round(pounds, 3)
    return str(pounds)
```

The first step is to analyze the requirements and dependencies for the code to run correctly. In this example, we need to convert it to a web app by using Flask. Therefore, this will be our requirement to install. Write the requirements.txt, as in Listing 9-2.

Listing 9-2. requirements.txt code

FLASK

The second step is to write the Dockerfile, as in Listing 9-3. The base image will be python, setting and adding the working directory and setting the host address to 0.0.0.0 to be accessed from the Internet and not restricted on our localhost. Then install the libraries and dependencies that we write in our requirements file. Expose the container port and finally pass the parameters to run the app to the CMD command. This app will have only a web interface without a database in the back end.

Listing 9-3. Dockerfile

```
# Use an official Python runtime as a parent image
FROM python
# Set the working directory to /app
WORKDIR /app
Add . /app
ENV FLASK_APP=app.py
ENV FLASK_RUN_HOST=0.0.0.0
COPY requirements.txt requirements.txt
RUN pip install -r requirements.txt
EXPOSE 5000
COPY . .
CMD ["flask", "run"]
```

This Dockerfile is written to run on our Windows Server 2016. If it will run on Linux, there are some differences. In Linux, we can use the python:slim version because it is a Linux-based image and lighter one. However, if we try to run this fast python image on Windows, the Docker daemon will give us a manifest error as in Figure 9-3.

```
PS C:\Users\Administrator\firstapp> docker build -t friendlyhello .
Sending build context to Docker daemon    5.12kB
Step 1/7 : FROM python:2.7-slim
2.7-slim: Pulling from library/python
no matching manifest for windows/amd64 in the manifest list entries
```

Figure 9-3. *Manifest error*

Now, we need to change our Python app code to a web app and import Flask in it, as in Listing 9-4, and save it as app.py.

Listing 9-4. Our application code in app.py

```python
from flask import Flask
from flask import request

app = Flask(__name__)

@app.route("/")
def index():
    kg= request.args.get("kg", "")
    if kg:
        pounds= pounds_from(kg)
    else:
        pounds= ""
    return (
        """<form action="" method="get">
                <input type="text" name="kg">
                <input type="submit" value="Convert">
            </form>"""
        + "pounds= "+ pounds
    )

def pounds_from(kg):
    pounds= float(kg) * 2.2
    pounds= round(pounds, 3)
    return str(pounds)
if __name__ == "__main__":
    app.run(host="0.0.0.0", port=5000, debug=True)
```

Now, we have three files: requirements.txt, Dockerfile, and app.py. The next step is to build the Dockerfile and run it using docker build -t kgpoundconverter ., as in Figure 9-4.

```
$ docker build -t kgpoundconverter .
Sending build context to Docker daemon  8.704kB
Step 1/10 : FROM python
 ---> b999f1d939ed
Step 2/10 : WORKDIR /app
 ---> Using cache
 ---> e225f27bb060
Step 3/10 : ADD . /app
 ---> ce6c73d74fa3
Removing intermediate container d303d0765904
Step 4/10 : ENV FLASK_APP app.py
 ---> Running in 4dfdee61a54c
 ---> 12fc3c1ed6c0
Removing intermediate container 4dfdee61a54c
Step 5/10 : ENV FLASK_RUN_HOST 0.0.0.0
 ---> Running in d0c90a4de309
 ---> c9e1f7d4fe69
Removing intermediate container d0c90a4de309
Step 6/10 : COPY requirements.txt requirements.txt
 ---> c865c58465cf
Removing intermediate container 4c6859470e0e
Step 7/10 : RUN pip install -r requirements.txt
 ---> Running in 2598b5bef8c4
```

Figure 9-4. *Snippet of building the image*

Run the app using docker run --rm -p 4000:5000 --name test
kgpoundconverter, as in Figure 9-5.

```
$ docker run --rm -p 4000:5000 --name test kgpoundconverter
 * Serving Flask app 'app.py' (lazy loading)
 * Environment: production
   WARNING: This is a development server. Do not use it in a production deployment.
   Use a production WSGI server instead.
 * Debug mode: off
 * Running on all addresses.
   WARNING: This is a development server. Do not use it in a production deployment.
 * Running on http://172.29.160.247:5000 (Press CTRL+C to quit)
172.29.160.1 - - [12/Jan/2022 17:59:53] "GET / HTTP/1.1" 200 -
```

Figure 9-5. *Craft a container from the new image*

In Figure 9-5, the Docker daemon generates the IP for the running container. Copy it and paste in the browser to test the application. If you are using MacOS and Linux, open localhost:4000 to test the application. Enter any weight in kilograms and click Submit. The app will convert it to pounds, as in Figure 9-6.

Figure 9-6. *Test the application in the browser*

Remember that if you tried the host to be localhost or 127.0.0.1 instead of 0.0.0.0 and you are testing on a Windows machine, not a Linux one, the localhost will not be resolved, as in Figure 9-7, although the container is running correctly in the background. Try docker container ls or docker ps.

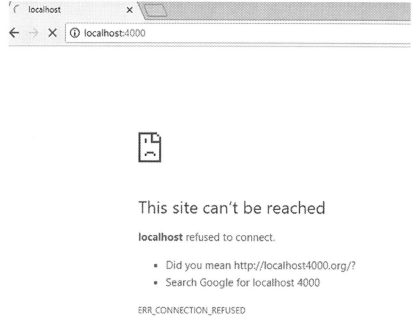

Figure 9-7. *Localhost cannot be resolved*

Again, there are some differences in networking between Windows and Linux:

- No bridge network.

- Localhost must be explicitly published .

If you try running docker network ls, the output is as Figure 9-8.

```
$ docker network ls
NETWORK ID          NAME            DRIVER          SCOPE
384fe1c44d0f        myswitch        transparent     local
45291ad0bcf7        nat             nat             local
0e69f8a789cf        none            null            local
```

Figure 9-8. *List the Docker networks on Windows*

If you ran the container as a daemon in the background, the IP address would not be displayed for you as in Figure 9-5. You can get the container's IP by inspecting it using docker inspect test. In the Networks section, the IP is displayed, as in Figure 9-9.

```
            "Networks": {
                "nat": {
                    "IPAMConfig": null,
                    "Links": null,
                    "Aliases": null,
                    "NetworkID": "335b24053bed45762fe6b861489f910ca8ba01faba7701
a44fb5ae3ece084527",
                    "EndpointID": "3aa5b28567d0ac4ecff09343d56e1f9465106c791d75f
5ef653a28053c90e53f",
                    "Gateway": "172.29.160.1",
                    "IPAddress": "172.29.160.247",
                    "IPPrefixLen": 16,
                    "IPv6Gateway": "",
                    "GlobalIPv6Address": "",
                    "GlobalIPv6PrefixLen": 0,
                    "MacAddress": "00:15:5d:b9:cf:63",
                    "DriverOpts": null
                }
            }
        }
    }
]
```

Figure 9-9. *The IPAddress in the Networks Section of the inspect subcommand output*

Java Example

As we mentioned before, the language is not an issue. However, from my experience teaching the Docker Enterprise for Developers course since 2017, I know that developers prefer having examples in the languages that they use. You can write the kg–pound converter in Java and substitute the app.py from the previous example and rerun it in Java. Note that the base image Java is deprecated. It will work; however, it is better to use openjdk as the base image in the Dockerfile.

To try other more advanced examples in Java where there are docker-compose files, try the following dockersamples/javarr-demo example, which is a public archive. The link is https://github.com/dockersamples/javaee-demo. This example needs a Linux machine; therefore, we will run it on a virtual machine like the ones that we created in Chapter 6.

First, we need to SSH our virtual machine using docker-machine ssh <machine name, e.g. again>. To git clone the code, use git clone https://github.com/dockersamples/javaee-demo.git. List the folder contents and open the javaee-demo folder, as in Figure 9-10.

```
docker@again:~$ git clone https://github.com/dockersamples/javaee-demo.git
Cloning into 'javaee-demo'...
remote: Enumerating objects: 8949, done.
remote: Total 8949 (delta 0), reused 0 (delta 0), pack-reused 8949
Receiving objects: 100% (8949/8949), 15.24 MiB | 8.45 MiB/s, done.
Resolving deltas: 100% (1858/1858), done.
Checking connectivity... done.
docker@again:~$ ls
javaee-demo
docker@again:~$ cd javaee-demo/
docker@again:~/javaee-demo$ ./add_pwd_host.sh
docker@again:~/javaee-demo$ ls
README.md                 add_pwd_host.sh          kube-deployment.yml
add_ee_kube_pwd_host.sh   docker-compose.yml       movieplex7
add_ee_pwd_host.sh        docker-stack-local.yml   original-solution
add_ee_swarm_pwd_host.sh  docker-stack.yml         react-client
```

Figure 9-10. *Explore the application contents and code*

Read the stack YML file using the cat docker-stack.yml command, as in Figure 9-11.

```
docker@again:~/javaee-demo$ cat docker-stack.yml
version: "3.2"

services:
  movieplex7:
    image: dockersamples/movieplex7-tomee
    ports:
      - "8080:8080"
    networks:
      - www
    deploy:
      replicas: 2
      update_config:
        parallelism: 2
        failure_action: rollback
      restart_policy:
        condition: on-failure
        delay: 5s
        max_attempts: 3
        window: 120s

  react-client:
    image: dockersamples/react-client
    ports:
      - "80:80"
    networks:
      - www
    deploy:
      replicas: 2
      update_config:
        parallelism: 2
        failure_action: rollback
      restart_policy:
        condition: on-failure
        delay: 5s
        max_attempts: 3
        window: 120s

networks:
    www:
```

Figure 9-11. *Cat the stack YML file*

Figure 9-11 shows that the application has two services: movieplex7 and react-client. The first service uses the movieplex7-tomee image, and the second one uses react-client. Copy the code, go to the UCP, click Create Stack, and paste the code. The UCP will download the images and create the services for us, as in Figure 9-12.

Figure 9-12. *Create a stack, and the services will be created for you*

Click Inspect the service, copy the IP address, and paste it in the browser, as in Figure 9-13. You can also check it using the CURL command.

Client application for JavaEE Movieplex MTA example

Figure 9-13. *Explore the application in the browser*

To verify that the Tomcat is installed correctly, in the browser write http://<VM IP address>:8080, as in Figure 9-14.

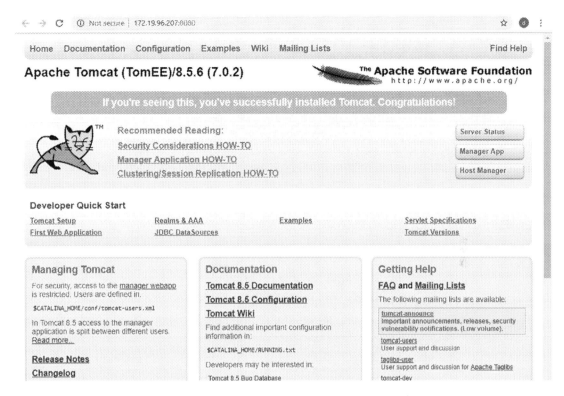

Figure 9-14. *Tomcat service*

.NET Example

If you are interested, please follow the following tutorial:

www.youtube.com/watch?v=a8Z3MncihLg

Extra Resources for .NET Tools

- https://docs.docker.com/engine/examples/dotnetcore/

- https://docs.microsoft.com/en-us/dotnet/core/docker/
  docker-basics-dotnet-core

- https://developercommunity.visualstudio.com/content/
  problem/313297/visual-studio-not-creating-docker-compose-
  project.html

- `https://docs.microsoft.com/en-us/dotnet/standard/
  containerized-lifecycle-architecture/design-develop-
  containerized-apps/visual-studio-tools-for-docker`

- `https://github.com/dotnet-architecture/eShopModernizing/
  wiki/02.-How-to-containerize-the-.NET-Framework-web-apps-
  with-Windows-Containers-and-Docker`

- Docker Reference Architecture – Development Pipeline Best
  Practices Using Docker EE: `https://success.docker.com/article/
  dev-pipeline`

Ebook

- `https://blogs.msdn.microsoft.com/cesardelatorre/2017/05/10/
  free-ebookguide-on-net-microservices-architecture-for-
  containerized-net-applications/`

Extra Examples

- `https://github.com/docker/labs`

- `https://github.com/dockersamples`

- `https://runnable.com/docker/java/dockerize-your-java-
  application`

- `https://github.com/docker/labs/blob/master/developer-
  tools/java/chapters/ch03-build-image.adoc`

- `https://alexandrnikitin.github.io/blog/running-java-inside-
  windows-container-on-windows-server/`

- `www.atlassian.com/blog/git/deploy-java-apps-with-
  docker-awesome`

- `https://docs.docker.com/engine/swarm/secrets/#simple-
  example-use-secrets-in-a-windows-service`

Summary

This chapter is not included in the DCA exam. However, understanding the monolithic vs. the microservices is the foundation of Docker and the main reason everyone is dockerizing/containerizing their applications. This chapter showed how to do that. From my experience, my students and clients are usually asking for the languages listed in the chapter.

CHAPTER 10

Orchestration

In this chapter, you will learn about how to go to production. It is all about services and writing the YAML file, whether you use the Docker swarm or Kubernetes as your orchestrator.

Therefore, the chapter will cover the following topics:

- The steps from development to production

- How to write a docker-compose YAML file

- How to write a Kubernetes manifest YAML file

From Development to Production

As we have seen in previous chapters, we start our app development by writing the code of every container independently with its Dockerfile to ensure that the required dependencies and libraries will be installed and running correctly, as in Figure 10-1.

121

© Engy Fouda 2022
E. Fouda, *A Complete Guide to Docker for Operations and Development*,
https://doi.org/10.1007/978-1-4842-8117-8_10

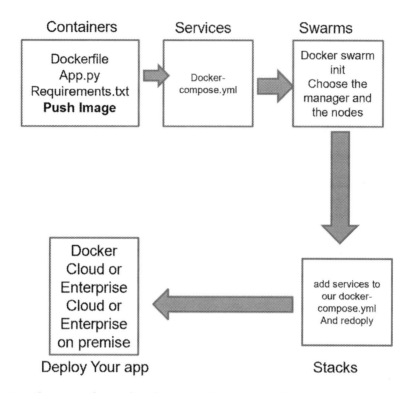

Figure 10-1. *The steps from development to production*

Then we encapsulate all that in an image and push it to a registry. When we want to put these pieces together to complete the puzzle, we write a YAML file to orchestrate between these services. Going to production and scaling, we elevate the level one step to services. Each service will be crafted from that image and specify other required options and replicas if needed to meet our customers' needs.

In short, services are containers in production. The stacks are a group of interrelated services that share dependencies and can be scaled together. This level is the top level of the distributed system hierarchy.

We will learn how to write YAML files for swarm and Kubernetes orchestrators in the coming sections. It is worth mentioning that there are other orchestrators in the market. However, these are the only two included in the DCA exam.

The YAML files for both the swarm services and the Kubernetes services have a standard feature, which is being divided into sections/top keys. These top keys are identified with a tab or two spaces per section, similar to Python, where the subsections are in the format of key: value. The value can be a filename or extend over more than one line. We usually write one file for the swarm that sets up the whole application. On the other hand, in Kubernetes, we write a file for every object. We can combine them in one file with three dashes between the objects' definitions.

How to Write a Swarm docker-compose YAML File?

The YAML file for a swarm consists basically of the following five top-level keys:

1. version: Indicates the version of the Compose file format. The value must be 3.0 or higher to work with stacks.

2. services: Where all the action occurs. We define the services that make the stack.

3. networks: We list the required networks.

4. secrets: We list the required secrets for the app to operate correctly.

5. volumes: If the application is stateful, we define the volumes needed by the services in this key.

We do not need to have all of them in our YAML file. We will have the keys we need for our application to operate correctly.

Let us have an example to demonstrate all this information. The application is called Example Voting App: https://github.com/dockersamples/example-voting-app. This example is licensed for public use. It is a simple distributed application running across multiple Docker containers and is prepared to be orchestrated using swarm and Kubernetes. The app allows users to vote between cats and dogs and displays the result.

The app consists of five services, as shown in its architecture, as in Figure 10-2. There is a front-end web app, voting-app, in Python, which lets us vote between cats and dogs. It can be accessed at port 5000. A Redis service collects new votes. A .NET Core worker service consumes votes and stores them. A PostgreSQL database backed by a Docker volume adds up the votes. Another front-end Node.js web app shows the results of the voting in real time and can be accessed at port 5001. As we see, we can combine services written in different programming languages.

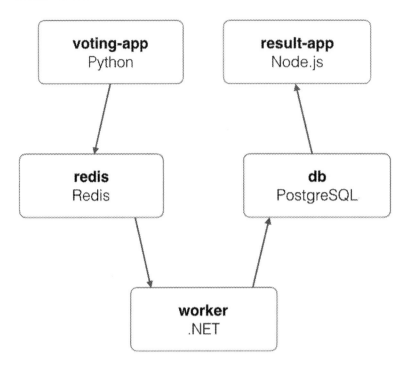

Figure 10-2. *Example Voting App architecture*

Now, let us look at the docker-compose.yml file, as in Listing 10-1. In this file, we have three top keys: services, volumes, and networks. In services, we have vote, result, worker, redis, and db.

In all of them, we specify the image. In development, we can use the `build` keyword as shown here. However, in production, we must build the images, push them to a registry, and substitute the `build` with the `image` keyword.

We will not explain all the services' sub-keys in detail. Let us have the vote service as an example; the app specifies the commands, dependencies, volumes, and port 5000 at the host and 80 at the container and the networks. The rest of the services are almost self-explanatory.

Listing 10-1. Example Voting App docker-compose.yml file

```
services:
      vote:
        build: ./vote
        # use python rather than gunicorn for local dev
        command: python app.py
```

```yaml
    depends_on:
      redis:
        condition: service_healthy
    volumes:
     - ./vote:/app
    ports:
      - "5000:80"
    networks:
      - front-tier
      - back-tier

result:
  build: ./result
  # use nodemon rather than node for local dev
  command: nodemon server.js
  depends_on:
    db:
      condition: service_healthy
  volumes:
    - ./result:/app
  ports:
    - "5001:80"
    - "5858:5858"
  networks:
    - front-tier
    - back-tier

worker:
  build:
    context: ./worker
  depends_on:
    redis:
      condition: service_healthy
    db:
      condition: service_healthy
  networks:
    - back-tier
```

```
redis:
  image: redis:5.0-alpine3.10
  volumes:
    - "./healthchecks:/healthchecks"
  healthcheck:
    test: /healthchecks/redis.sh
    interval: "5s"
  ports: ["6379"]
  networks:
    - back-tier

db:
  image: postgres:9.4
  environment:
    POSTGRES_USER: "postgres"
    POSTGRES_PASSWORD: "postgres"
  volumes:
    - "db-data:/var/lib/postgresql/data"
    - "./healthchecks:/healthchecks"
  healthcheck:
    test: /healthchecks/postgres.sh
    interval: "5s"
  networks:
    - back-tier

volumes:
  db-data:

networks:
  front-tier:
  back-tier:
```

How to Write a Kubernetes Manifest YAML File?

In Kubernetes terminology, the services in the swarm are called apps. Every app in the application architecture mentioned in Figure 10-2 must have two manifest YAML files to define its objects. One object is the deployment, and the other is for service, as in Figure 10-3. All apps must have the same namespace. Therefore, as in Figure 10-2, there is only one namespace file. The link for this folder is `https://github.com/dockersamples/example-voting-app/tree/master/k8s-specifications`.

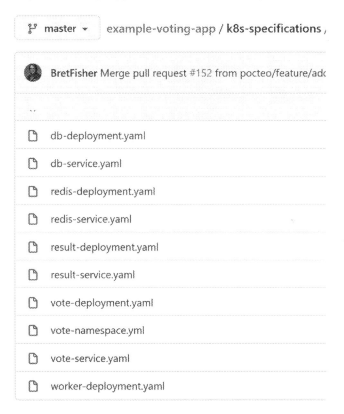

Figure 10-3. *The Kubernetes' file specifications*

The main top keys in the Kubernetes manifest YML file are these four top keys:

1. apiversion: Indicates the version of the manifest file.

2. kind: Specifies the object type, for example, pod, deployment, service, namespace, persistent volume, persistent volume claim, or storage class.

3. metadata: This key is crucial because it defines the labels. The name of the app is one of the labels. We can define more than one label for the object. Also, in metadata, we define the namespace name.

4. spec: This is where the action is. In this top key, we define the replicas, the selector, and the template. Inside the template, we can define the image where the container will be crafted from, ports, and any other specifications to run the application correctly.

Let us inspect the code of one app, vote, and see its namespace, deployment, and service manifest files in Listings 10-2, 10-3, and 10-4. The other apps of redis, result, worker, and db are similar in format as the vote one.

We use namespaces to allow several projects to share the same Kubernetes cluster. Therefore, Kubernetes needs namespaces to know the interconnected apps that are communicating with each other and isolate them from other projects. In other words, namespaces divide the cluster into interconnected sub-clusters.

To define it, as in Listing 10-2, we need only three top keys from the mentioned preceding list. We define the apiversion, and the kind of this object is the namespace, and the metadata has a sub-key, name, that has the value of vote that will be used in all the other files as we will see examples later.

Listing 10-2. vote namespace YML file

```
apiVersion: v1
kind: Namespace
metadata:
  name: vote
```

In general, deployments are responsible for self-healing and scalability. Kubernetes automatically creates pods' replicas and replica sets in the background without us explicitly writing their code. Deployments manage replica sets, and replica sets manage pods.

To define the deployment YML file, as in Listing 10-3, we need to define all the preceding top keys. The kind this time is deployment. In the metadata key, we define the labels to have the namespace as vote and the app name and name as vote. However, when we check the redis files, for example, the app name and name are redis, not

vote. The link for the redis deployment file is https://github.com/dockersamples/
example-voting-app/blob/master/k8s-specifications/redis-deployment.yaml. For
the spec, the replicas are only one, and the selector has the matchlabels ➤ labels
➤ app is vote. The subsection spec identifies the image for creating the container, the
container's name, and port.

Listing 10-3. vote deployment YML file

```
apiVersion: apps/v1
kind: Deployment
metadata:
  labels:
    app: vote
  name: vote
  namespace: vote
spec:
  replicas: 1
  selector:
    matchLabels:
      app: vote
  template:
    metadata:
      labels:
        app: vote
    spec:
      containers:
      - image: dockersamples/examplevotingapp_vote:before
        name: vote
        ports:
        - containerPort: 80
          name: vote
```

A Kubernetes service uses labels as nametags to identity pods, and it can query
based on these labels for service discovery and load-balancing. In Chapter 4, we
discussed the Kubernetes service in detail.

Listing 10-4. vote service YML file

```
apiVersion: v1
kind: Service
metadata:
  labels:
    app: vote
  name: vote
  namespace: vote
spec:
  type: NodePort
  ports:
  - name: "vote-service"
    port: 5000
    targetPort: 80
    nodePort: 31000
  selector:
    app: vote
```

Now, after we understood how all these pieces fall together, let us run the code, see the project in action, vote on the browser, and see the voting result. To do that, we need to git clone the code, install docker-compose, and run the application using the docker-compose up command, as in Listing 10-5. Later, we will check the output in the browser.

Listing 10-5. Clone the application, install docker-compose, and run the application

```
git clone https://github.com/dockersamples/example-voting-app

sudo curl -L "https://github.com/docker/compose/releases/download/1.29.2/
docker-compose-$(uname -s)-$(uname -m)" -o /usr/local/bin/docker-compose
sudo chmod +x /usr/local/bin/docker-compose
docker-compose up
```

When we run the docker-compose up, Docker will build the images and run the containers for us. This step is for testing in development before going to production to see if anything might fail, if any code generates an error, and if there is a missing library. The output will start as in Figure 10-4; for this step, we do not need a swarm, and we can use the Docker CE to perform it.

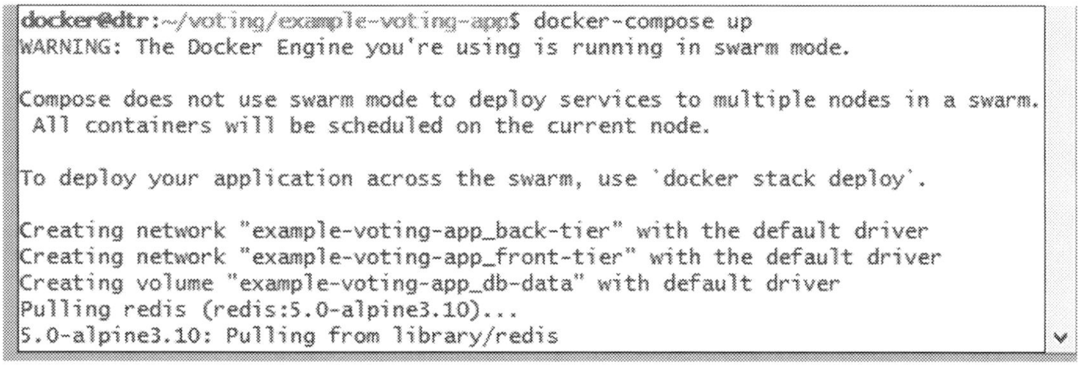

```
docker@dtr:~/voting/example-voting-app$ docker-compose up
WARNING: The Docker Engine you're using is running in swarm mode.

Compose does not use swarm mode to deploy services to multiple nodes in a swarm.
 All containers will be scheduled on the current node.

To deploy your application across the swarm, use 'docker stack deploy'.

Creating network "example-voting-app_back-tier" with the default driver
Creating network "example-voting-app_front-tier" with the default driver
Creating volume "example-voting-app_db-data" with default driver
Pulling redis (redis:5.0-alpine3.10)...
5.0-alpine3.10: Pulling from library/redis
```

Figure 10-4. *Run docker-compose up*

When everything is up and running, as in Figure 10-5, we see a replica of several services as db_1, result_1, vote_1, and worker_1. After a while, it will show redis_1 as well, and the services will be waiting for any request from the browser to start the execution.

```
db_1        | waiting for server to shut down....LOG:  database system is shut dow
n
db_1        |  done
db_1        | server stopped
db_1        |
db_1        | PostgreSQL init process complete; ready for start up.
db_1        |
db_1        | LOG:  database system was shut down at 2022-01-20 02:22:53 UTC
db_1        | LOG:  MultiXact member wraparound protections are now enabled
db_1        | LOG:  database system is ready to accept connections
db_1        | LOG:  autovacuum launcher started
result_1    | [nodemon] 2.0.15
result_1    | [nodemon] to restart at any time, enter `rs`
result_1    | [nodemon] watching path(s): *.*
result_1    | [nodemon] watching extensions: js,mjs,json
result_1    | [nodemon] starting `node server.js`
              Connected to db
              Found redis at 172.20.0.2
              Connecting to redis
result_1    | Thu, 20 Jan 2022 02:23:03 GMT body-parser deprecated bodyParser: use
 individual json/urlencoded middlewares at server.js:73:9
result_1    | Thu, 20 Jan 2022 02:23:03 GMT body-parser deprecated undefined exten
ded: provide extended option at ../node_modules/body-parser/index.js:105:29
result_1    | App running on port 80
result_1    | Connected to db
vote_1      | 172.19.118.13 - - [20/Jan/2022 02:30:18] "GET / HTTP/1.1" 200 -
vote_1      | 172.19.118.13 - - [20/Jan/2022 02:30:18] "GET /static/stylesheets/st
yle.css HTTP/1.1" 200 -
vote_1      | 172.19.118.13 - - [20/Jan/2022 02:30:19] "GET /favicon.ico HTTP/1.1"
 404 -
vote_1      | [2022-01-20 02:30:29,193] INFO in app: Received vote for a
vote_1      | 172.19.118.13 - - [20/Jan/2022 02:30:29] "POST / HTTP/1.1" 200 -
```

Figure 10-5. *One replica from every service*

To access the project, go to the browser, as in Figure 10-6, and enter http://<the machine IP>/5000 in the address. If the machine is Linux, the address http://localhost:5000 will work, too.

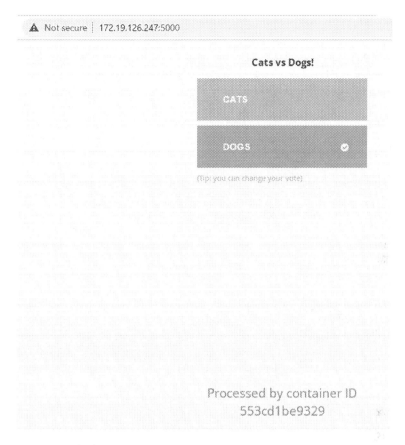

Figure 10-6. *Vote web-front at port 5000*

To see the result, open a new tab and enter the address as http://<the machine IP>:5001, as in Figure 10-7.

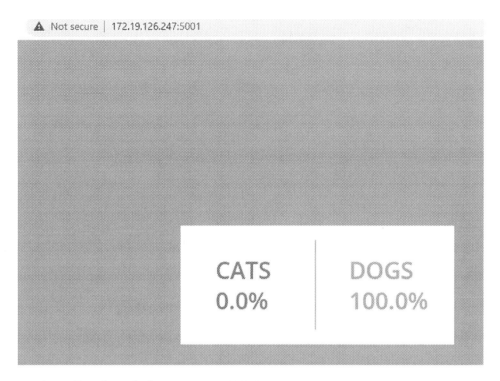

Figure 10-7. *Result web-front at port 5001*

To take down the whole project, run docker-compose down. The daemon will delete the networks and remove any objects from the host for us. As we have seen in this project, we usually write several YAML files to suit the development, testing, and swarm/Kubernetes orchestration in production.

Summary

This chapter talked about how to orchestrate between your application's containers. There are several orchestrators in the market. However, the DCA exam focuses only on swarm and Kubernetes. Therefore, the chapter discussed the process from coding to production and how to write the docker-compose YAML file and the Kubernetes manifest YAML file.

CHAPTER 11

Security

In this chapter, you will learn about the security features in the Enterprise Edition. One of the most crucial security features in Docker and Kubernetes is the Role-Based Access Control. You will practice with hands-on lab exercises. Also, this chapter discusses secrets, Docker Content Trust (DCT), and Transport Layer Security (TLS). The tricky questions in the exam usually focus on DCT, TLS, and the secrets.

Therefore, the chapter will cover the following topics:

- Role-Based Access Control (RBAC)

- Secrets

- Docker Content Trust (DCT)

Role-Based Access Control (RBAC)

The Role-Based Access Control (RBAC) in the Docker EE is granular and powerful. It is done by creating grants. As in Figure 11-1, the grant consists of

1. Subject

2. Collection

3. Role

Grant		
Subject	**Role**	**Resource Sets**
Team-masters	**mastersecrests**	**/masters/kubeadmins**

Figure 11-1. Grant consists of subject, role, and resource sets

The subject is the team or one or more users who will access a certain collection/ resource with granular roles/privileges. After creating the three objects mentioned earlier individually, you create a grant that combines all of them. You can make the grant and its components using the UCP or the command line. RBAC is from the best practices that everyone must follow and is created in Docker and Kubernetes in the same way. You can know more about Kubernetes security from CNCF: www.cncf.io/ blog/2019/01/14/9-kubernetes-security-best-practices-everyone-must-follow/.

Create a Subject

In this example, we will create a "masters" team that needs to access all the swarm secrets' operations. First, we need to create some users and group them in a team and call it masters. In the left panel, click User Management ➤ Users. In the right panel, click Create User, as in Figure 11-2.

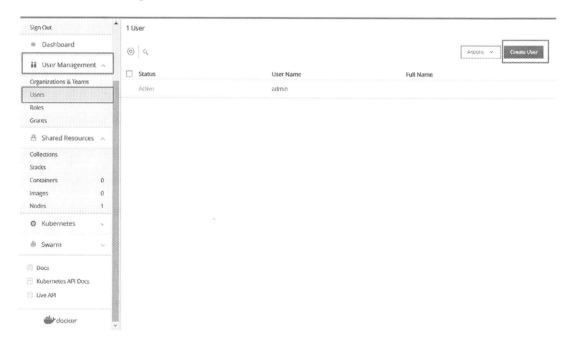

Figure 11-2. *Create a new user*

In the following screen, enter the username, password, and full name. Let the username and full name be "master1." Then click Create, as in Figure 11-3.

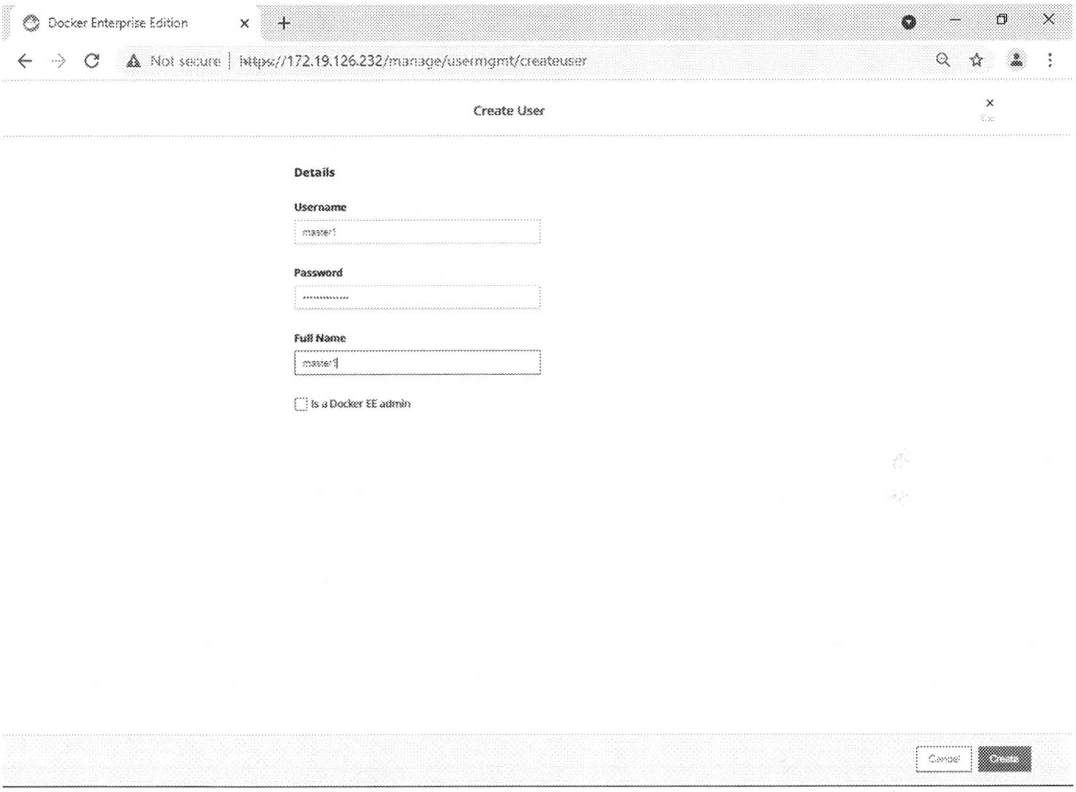

Figure 11-3. *Enter the user's credentials*

The UCP UI displays a user list with the new user in it and a message that the user has been created successfully. If there is any error generated, the UCP will generate for you an error message. Repeat the steps to create another user, master2, as in Figure 11-4.

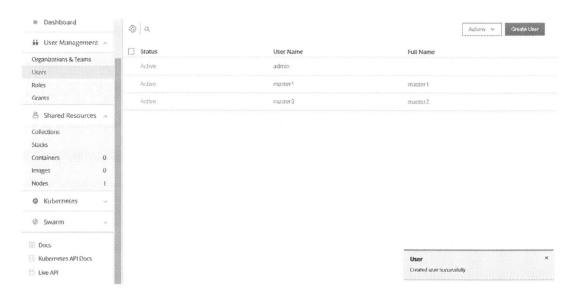

Figure 11-4. *Create another user*

Now, let us create an organization and a team. Then add the two users to that team. On the left, click User Management ➤ Organizations and Teams ➤ Create Organization. Write the organization's name as "kuber-masters" and click the Create button, as in Figure 11-5. Automatically, the UCP UI lists the organization names, and a message says that the organization has been created successfully.

Figure 11-5. *Create a new organization*

On the right of the organization's name, click the three vertical dots. Select from the menu Add Team, as in Figure 11-6.

Figure 11-6. *Add a team to the organization*

Enter the team details: the Team Name and Description, as in Figure 11-7. For this exercise, let us call the team "masters."

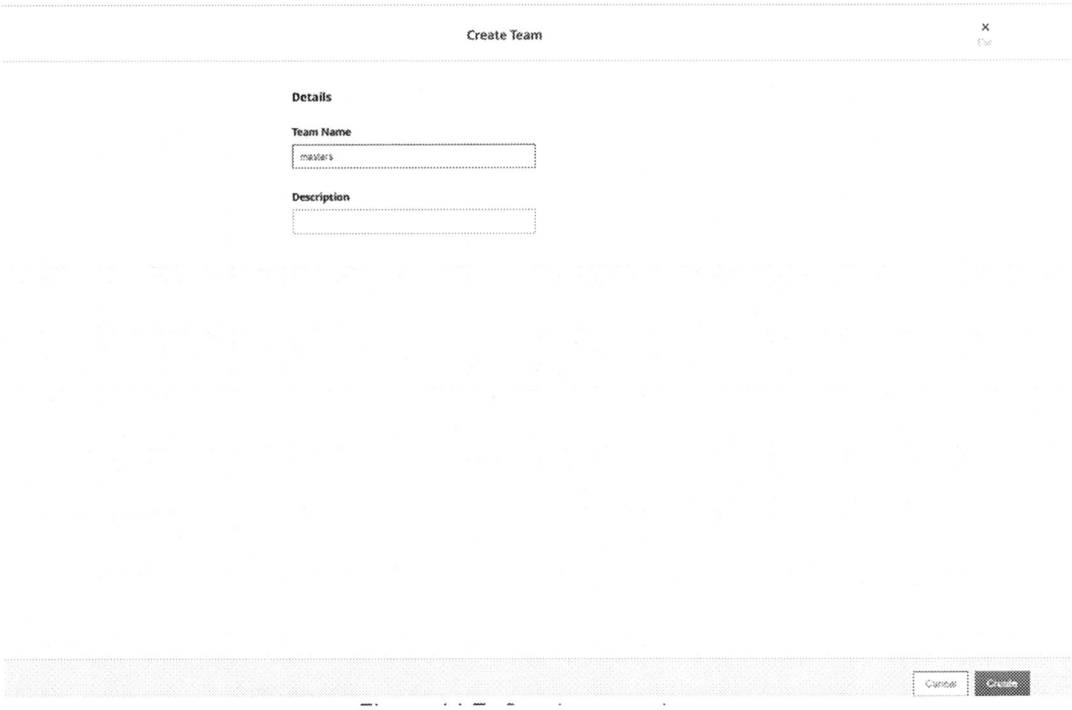

Figure 11-7. *Create a new team*

As before, the UCP displays the organization's team list and states that the team was created successfully, as in Figure 11-8.

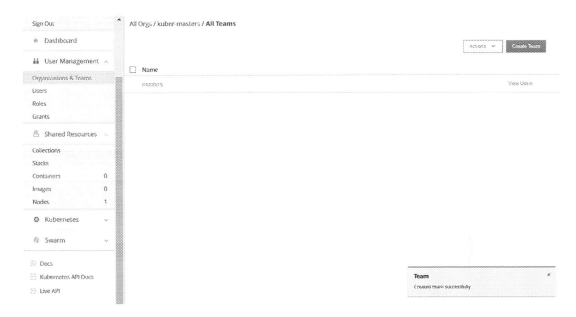

Figure 11-8. *Team list*

Now that we created the organization and team, we need to add the users that we created at the beginning to this team. Click the three vertical dots on the right of the team's name and select Add User from the menu, as in Figure 11-9.

Figure 11-9. *Add users to the team*

Select the user to add to the team and click Add Users, as in Figure 11-10.

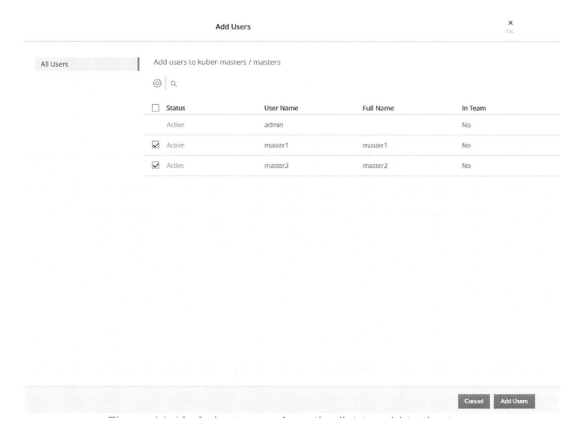

Figure 11-10. *Select users from the list to add to the team*

Again, the UCP displays a note that says the users have been added to the team.

Create a Collection

Now, we are done with the first step of creating a grant. The plan is to create users, a collection, a role, and a grant. The best practice is not to assign a role and collection to users but to teams. Therefore, we created an organization and a team and added users to it.

The second step is to create a collection. In the left panel, click Shared Resources ➤ Collections. On the right, click Create Collection, as in Figure 11-11.

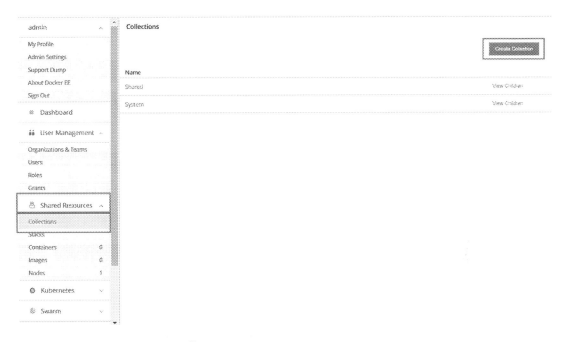

Figure 11-11. *Create a collection*

Enter the name of the collection as masters, as in Figure 11-12. Collection can be created as trees where the parents have access to all their children and not vice versa. For this example, we shall create one parent and one child and assign the secret to the child.

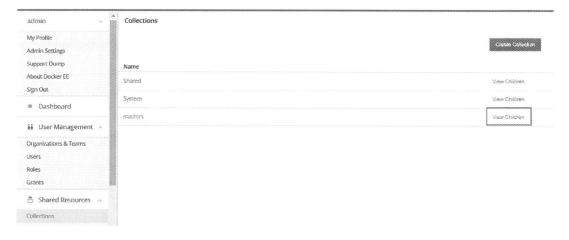

| Create Collection: / | × |

Details
Label Constraints

🗄 **Collections and Namespaces**

Docker EE enables controlling access to swarm resources by using collections and Kubernetes resources with namespaces.

Access to collections and namespaces goes through a directory structure that arranges a swarm's resources. To assign permissions, administrators create grants against directory branches

Learn More

Details

Collection Name

masters

Cancel   Create

Figure 11-12. *Create a parent collection*

Click View Children, as in Figure 11-13, to create the child.

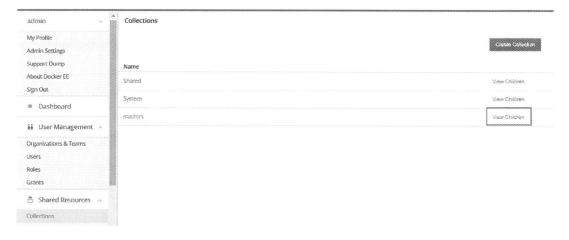

Figure 11-13. *Click View Children*

As in Figure 11-14, the UCP displays that it does not have any children. Click Create Collection to create one.

Figure 11-14. *Create a child collection*

Create a child collection called kubeadmins. Then click Create, as in Figure 11-15.

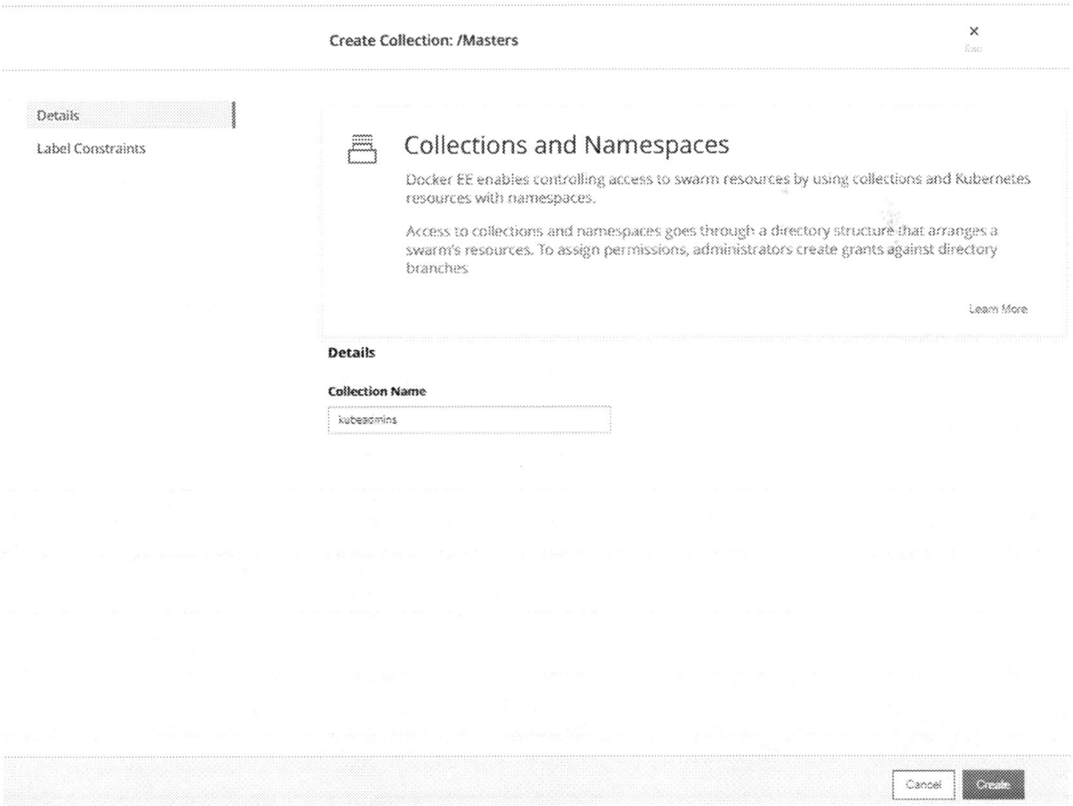

Figure 11-15. *Name the child collection*

You can create as many grandchildren as you need. As in Figure 11-16, you can click View Children and create more child collections. However, for this example, you will stop at this step. The RBAC is so granular.

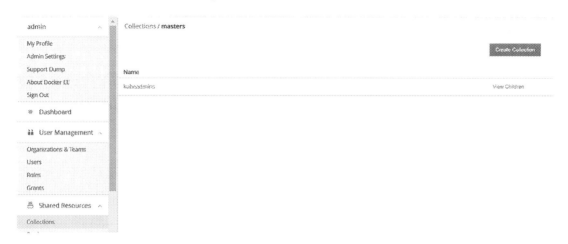

Figure 11-16. *You can create a grandchild collection*

For this example, the resource is a secret, and we will add it to the kubeadmins collection. Create a secret by clicking the Swarm tab in the left panel. When it expands, click Secrets. The UCP will list all the secrets that you have, if you have any. In our example, as in Figure 11-17, we do not have any secrets. Click Create Secret.

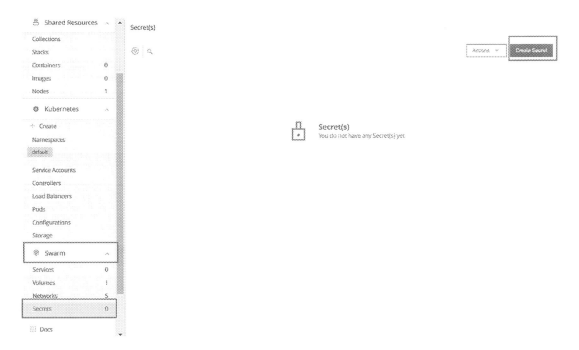

Figure 11-17. *Create a secret*

Enter the secret name as masterssecret, as in Figure 11-18. Also, enter the secret's content, which can be any content that can be sensitive data that you want to save. The secret contents get encrypted and cannot be decrypted after creation. For this example, enter any random letters. Remember that this content cannot be retrieved after being created. In case you forgot this data, your only solution is to delete the secret and create a new one.

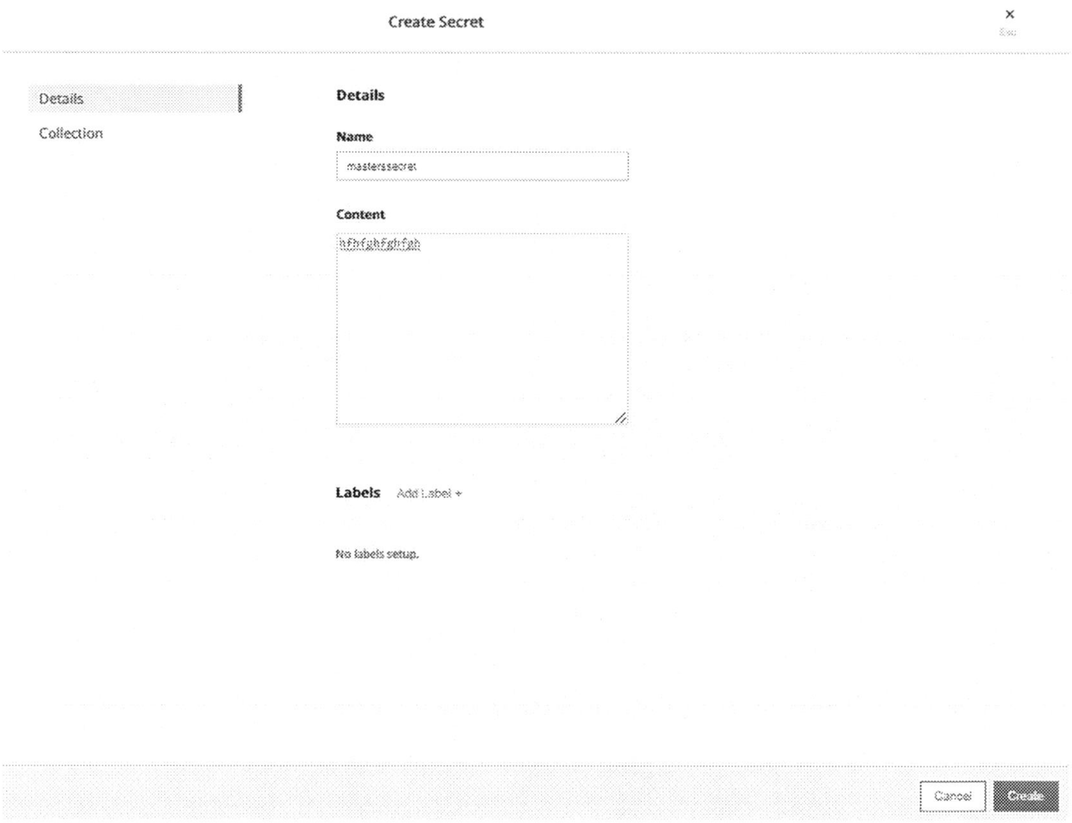

Create Secret   ×
                                                                             Esc

Details   **Details**
Collection   **Name**

                           masterssecret

                           Content

                           hfhfghfghfah

                           Labels   Add Label +

                           No labels setup.

                                                                Cancel   Create

Figure 11-18. *Enter the secret information*

On the left, click Collection and click Swarm ➤ View Children till you reach the level that you want, as in Figure 11-19. In our case, kubeadmins will be our level.

Create Secret   ×
                                                                             Esc

Details   Name
Collection   Swarm   View Children   Selected

Figure 11-19. *Add the resource to the collection branch level*

Click View Children in front of masters, as in Figure 11-20.

Figure 11-20. *Click View Children*

When you reach the level that you want, click Select Collection, as in Figure 11-21. Do not forget to click Create at the bottom to create the secret.

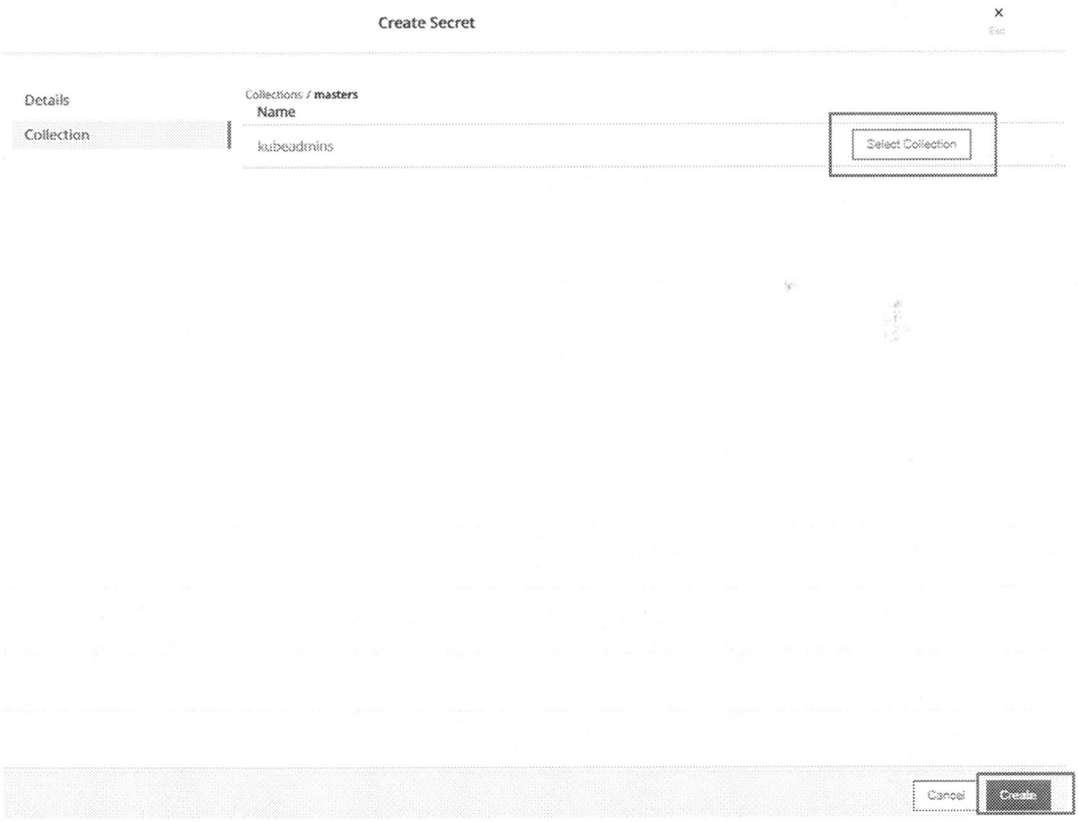

Figure 11-21. *Select the collection and create the secret*

The UCP displays a note saying that the secret has been created successfully, as in Figure 11-22.

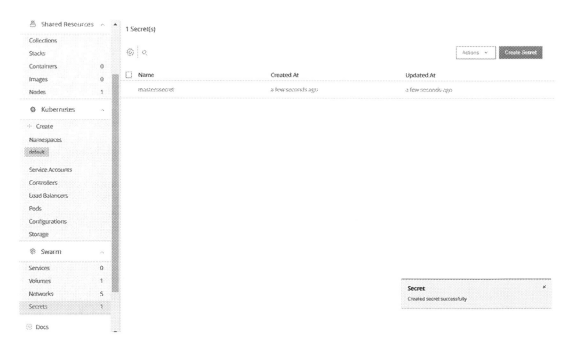

Figure 11-22. *Our secret has been added to the collection and created successfully*

Create a Role

According to our plan, we finished creating the users and the collection. The third step is to create a role, which represents the privileges to a resource. We will create a role to grant all secret privileges to the masters team. On the left, select User Management ➤ Roles ➤ Create Role, as in Figure 11-23.

Figure 11-23. *Create a role*

Enter the role name as masterssecrets, as in Figure 11-24.

Figure 11-24. *Enter the role name*

On the left, select Operations to select the privileges. In this example, we will grant all secret operations. When you are done, click Create, as in Figure 11-25.

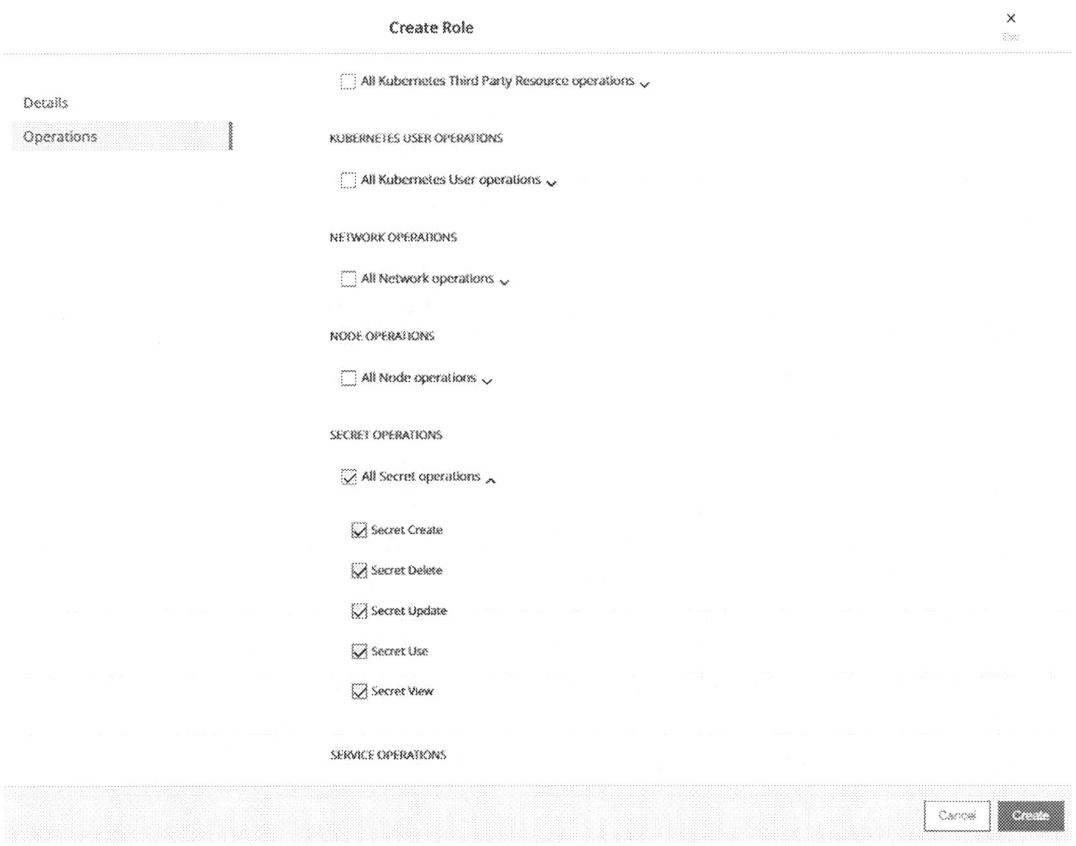

Figure 11-25. *Select all secret operations*

Again, the UCP displays that the role has been created successfully, as in Figure 11-26.

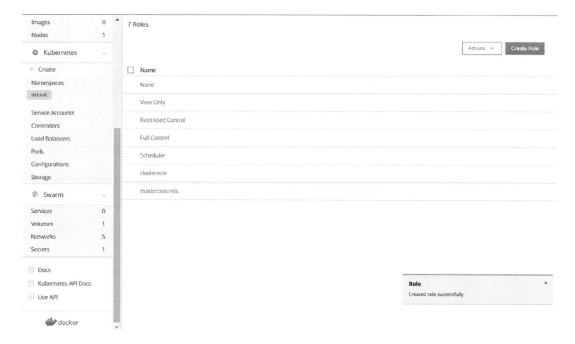

Figure 11-26. *The role has been created successfully*

Create a Grant

Since we have our subject, collection, and role ready, we combine all of them in a grant. This is our final step in the RBAC. On the left, select User Management ➤ Grants. You might find some grants already created for administrative purposes. On the right, click Create Grant to create a new one, as in Figure 11-27.

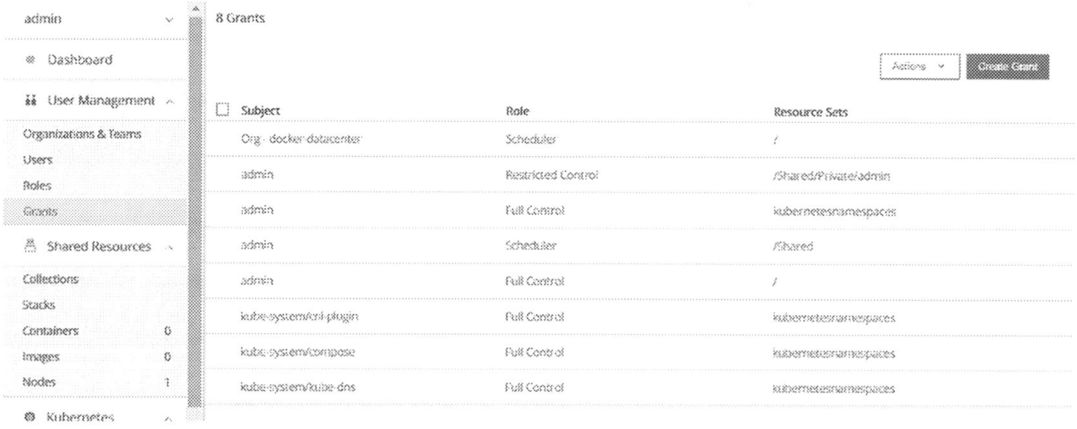

Figure 11-27. *Create Grant*

The UCP will display a help description for you that says, "A grant defines who (subject) has how much access (role) to a set of resources (collection). Each grant is a 1:1:1 mapping of subject, role, and collection." For our example, the masters team will have access to all secret operations in the kubeadmins collection.

Figure 11-28 shows these three options on the left: Resource Sets, Roles, and Subjects. The grant type is COLLECTIONS. Click View Children to see swarm child collections and select ours from them.

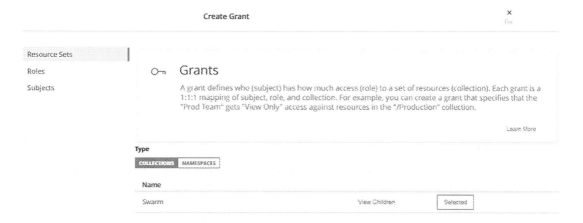

Figure 11-28. *In Resource Sets, select Collections*

The collection list is displayed. Click View Children of masters, as in Figure 11-29.

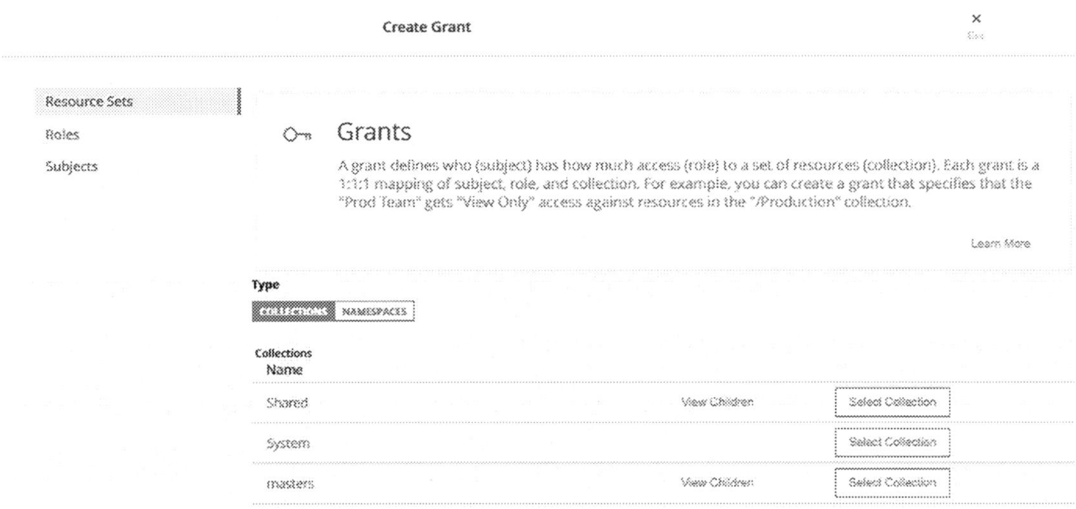

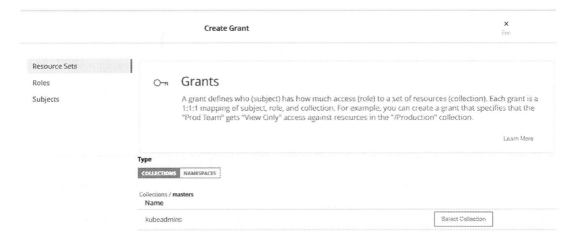

Figure 11-29. *View the masters child collection*

Select kubeadmins from the list by clicking Select Collection, as in Figure 11-30.

Figure 11-30. *Select the child collection*

On the left, click Roles and select masterssecrets from the drop-down menu, as in Figure 11-31.

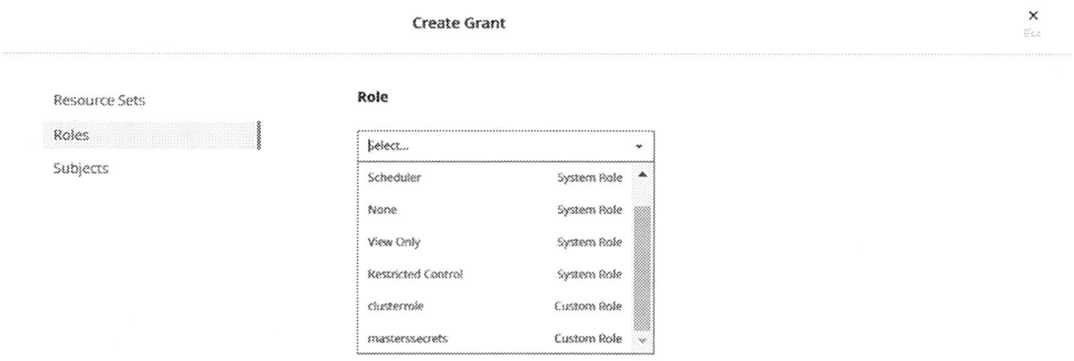

Figure 11-31. *Select masterssecrets*

Finally, on the left, click Subjects and select the kuber-masters organization and the masters team from the drop-down menus and click Create, as in Figure 11-32.

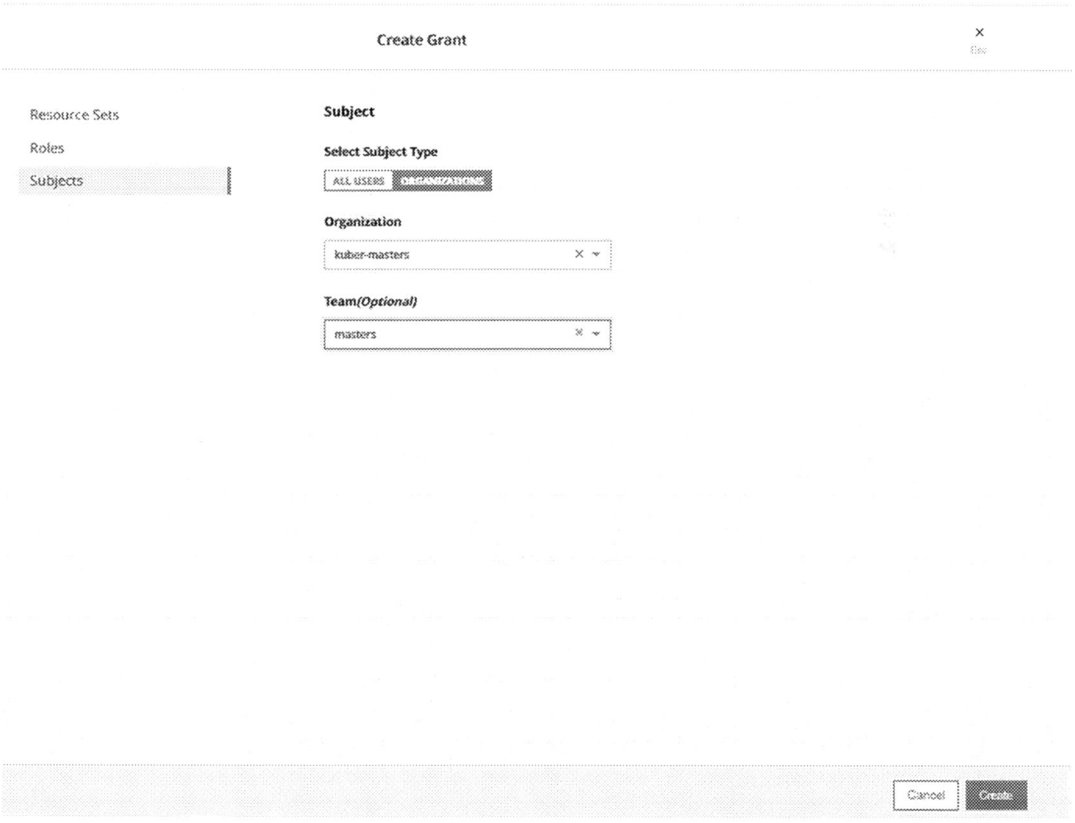

Figure 11-32. *Select an organization and team and click Create*

The UCP will pop to us a message saying that the grant has been successfully created, as in Figure 11-33.

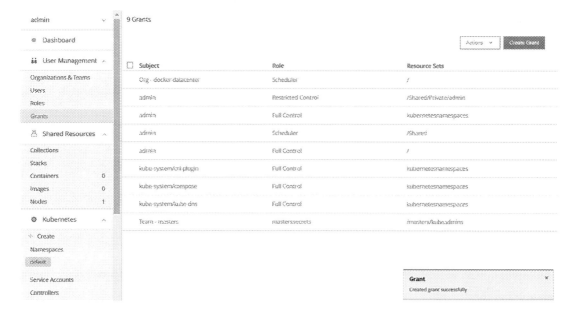

Figure 11-33. *The grant has been created successfully*

As you have seen in this section, you can assign very granular and precise privileges to each of Docker and Kubernetes objects to which teams. Always remember that the best practice is to assign the roles to teams and not to individual users as we have done in our example.

Docker Content Trust (DCT)

DCT is used to sign and verify the content digitally between senders, a Docker registry with an attached Notary server, and receivers. These signatures add to the trust and verification of images at the client.

Docker uses three keys:

- Root/offline key

- Repository/tagging key

- Timestamp key

There are two ways/sets of commands to create these keys. Let us demonstrate them with two examples.

Example 1:

1. Open your Git Bash window (MinGW64) and SSH any of your nodes by typing $`docker-machine ssh <VM name>` and click enter. The prompt will change to `docker@<VM name>:~$`.

2. Pull any image before setting the DCT value, for example, alpine or busybox, a small image:

   ```
   $ docker image pull busybox
   ```

3. Tag the image by your Docker username to be able to push it to your Docker Hub repo:

   ```
   $ docker image tag alpine:latest <Docker hub username>/trial:v2
   ```

4. Export the environment variable DOCKER_CONTENT_TRUST to 1:

   ```
   $ export DOCKER_CONTENT_TRUST=1
   ```

   It is case sensitive.

5. Docker login to your account using

   ```
   $ docker login
   ```

6. Push your new image to your Docker Hub, as in Figure 11-34:

   ```
   $ docker image push <Docker Hub username>/trial:v2
   ```

   A Docker host will ask you to create root and repository keys to attach them to the image.

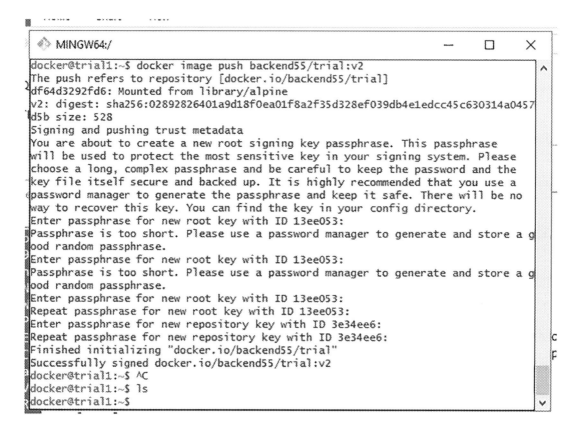

Figure 11-34. *Push the image after exporting the DOCKER_CONTENT_TRUST environment variable to 1*

Since setting the DOCKER_CONTENT_TRUST=1, all images pulled or pushed must be signed as shown in the previous step unless these images are official or verified images, as in Figure 11-35.

```
docker@trial1:~$ docker pull busybox
Using default tag: latest
Pull (1 of 1): busybox:latest@sha256:2a03a6059f21e150ae84b0973863609494aad70f0a8
0eaeb64bddd8d92465812
sha256:2a03a6059f21e150ae84b0973863609494aad70f0a80eaeb64bddd8d92465812: Pulling
 from library/busybox
90e01955edcd: Pull complete
Digest: sha256:2a03a6059f21e150ae84b0973863609494aad70f0a80eaeb64bddd8d92465812
Status: Downloaded newer image for busybox@sha256:2a03a6059f21e150ae84b097386360
9494aad70f0a80eaeb64bddd8d92465812
Tagging busybox@sha256:2a03a6059f21e150ae84b0973863609494aad70f0a80eaeb64bddd8d9
2465812 as busybox:latest
```

Figure 11-35. *Pull an official image and observe the difference from signing images*

If you try to pull an unverified image, the Docker host will refuse and will generate an error, as in Figure 11-36.

```
docker@trial1:~$ docker image pull backend55/database
Using default tag: latest
Error: remote trust data does not exist for docker.io/backend55/database: notary
.docker.io does not have trust data for docker.io/backend55/database
docker@trial1:~$
```

Figure 11-36. *Pull an unverified image*

Now to disable DCT, set its value to any number other than 1, for example:

```
$ export DOCKER_CONTENT_TRUST=0
```

The root key is the most crucial key. Do not lose it, or you will need a manual intervention from Docker Support to reset it, and this will be a big hassle and will cause delays to your system and customers. It belongs to one person or to an organization.

The repository key is associated with an image repository. The last key, the timestamp one, is for the image freshness.

Note   Some might try to work around the restriction by disabling DCT:

`$ docker image pull --disable-content-trust`. They will be able to pull unverified images. However, they will not be able to run them to create containers.

Example 2:

In this example, we will use the `$ docker trust` subcommands to create the keys:

```
$ docker trust key generate <your name>
$ docker trust signer add --key cert.pem <your name> <registry
address>/<username>/<image name>:<tag>
$ export DOCKER_CONTENT_TRUST=1
$ docker push <registry address>/<username>/<image name>:<tag>
```

To remove remote trust data, use the $docker trust revoke subcommand.

You can learn more about the second way from the Docker documentation: https://docs.docker.com/engine/security/trust/#signing-images-with-docker-content-trust.

In conclusion, the purpose of Docker Content Trust is to sign the images pulled and pushed from and to the Docker registries.

Transport Layer Security (TLS)

This section will not explain Transport Layer Security (TLS) in detail. It merely will focus on the points that the DCA exam asks about. TLS ensures authenticity of the registry endpoint and that traffic to/from registry is encrypted.

You use TLS (HTTPS) to protect the Docker daemon socket. If you need Docker to be reachable through HTTP rather than SSH in a safe manner, you can enable TLS (HTTPS) by specifying the tlsverify flag and pointing Docker's tlscacert flag to a trusted CA certificate.

To configure the Docker engine to use a registry that is not configured with TLS certificates from a trusted CA, pass the --insecure-registry flag to the dockerd daemon at runtime. Also, place the certificate in '/etc/docker/certs.d/dtr.example com/ca.crt' on all cluster nodes. These two steps will save you from receiving the error 'x509: certificate signed by unknown authority'.

To learn more about TLS, please check the following links from the Docker documentation:

https://docs.docker.com/engine/security/certificates/

https://docs.docker.com/engine/security/protect-access/#:~:text=Use%20TLS%20(HTTPS)%20to%20protect,to%20a%20trusted%20CA%20certificate.

```
https://docs.docker.com/registry/insecure/
```

```
https://docs.docker.com/engine/reference/commandline/
dockerd/
```

Summary

This chapter focused on the security section in the DCA exam. There are plenty of more topics that you need to learn to make sure that your Docker and Kubernetes are secure. This exam usually asks about the RBAC, TLS, DCA, and secrets. The RBAC is so easy to be done by the UCP UI. However, you can do all these steps using the CLI as well. For the exam, always remember the difference between DCA and TLS. The exam tries to confuse you about them.

CHAPTER 12

DCA Exam Requirements

This chapter provides the current exam requirements and guides you on how to register, the modalities, and the question types. However, all of these are subject to change at any time. Therefore, please check the exam website for the latest updates and changes to be on the safe side. The current website is `https://training.mirantis.com/dca-certification-exam/`.

Examination Format

The examination

- Contains 55 questions
    - 13 multiple-choice questions
    - 42 discrete option multiple-choice (DOMC) questions
- Takes 90 minutes
- Is remotely proctored on your Windows or Mac computer
- Costs $195 or €175 purchased online

Results per section are delivered immediately.

Pass the Exam Sections

In Chapter 1, we listed the exam sections and their weights. To pass the overall DCA exam, you must pass every section independently and score overall higher than 50%. If you failed any section, you fail the exam despite having an overall score of above average. Therefore, you must study for all the sections and never ignore any of them.

© Engy Fouda 2022
E. Fouda, *A Complete Guide to Docker for Operations and Development*,
https://doi.org/10.1007/978-1-4842-8117-8_12

Registration Link and Certification

You can register for your exam from this link:

    https://prod.examity.com/docker/

Your certification will be valid for 2 years. The exam modalities are in person and online.

If you do not pass a Docker certification exam, you may retake the exam, subject to the following conditions:

- Wait 14 days from the day you fail to take the exam again.

- Pay the exam price each time you attempt an exam.

After your attempt, take few minutes to write all the questions that you remember from the exam and try to look for the answers. We hope you will pass from your first trial. Please revise the quizzes listed in this book and the extra resources. Give yourself enough time to get prepared and do all examples by hand to gain the required experience and skills.

For Online Remotely Proctored Exams

On the day of your exam, be mindful of the testing environment requirements and check your system readiness before the exam time:

- Zoom desktop client

- A current version of Microsoft Windows or Mac OS X

- Google Chrome web browser and the ability to install a Chrome extension

- A web camera accessible by Google Chrome

Your proctor will start your session precisely at your appointment start time, so allow yourself enough time to log in to the Examity site before your appointment. Examity will send you an email that has the link. The proctor will ask to verify the following before starting the exam:

- Testing environment requirements.

- Web cam, speakers, and microphone must remain on throughout the exam.

- Alone in the room.

- Clear desk and area.

- Connected to a power source.

- No phones or headphones.

- No dual monitors.

- No leaving your seat.

- No talking.

- You cannot open any browser tab other than the exam one.

Question Types

There are two types of questions: the multiple-choice questions and the discrete option multiple-choice questions.

Multiple-Choice Questions

- Examinees are presented a question with at least four response options and must select one or more options to best answer the question.

- Distracters or wrong answers will be presented as response options.

- These are response options that examinees with incomplete knowledge or skill might choose, as they are generally plausible responses fitting into the content area defined by the test objective.

Discrete Option Multiple-Choice (DOMC) Questions

- DOMC items represent a relatively simple but useful change in the delivery of multiple-choice questions.

- Options are randomly presented, one at a time.

- For each presented option, the examinee chooses YES or NO to indicate if the option is correct.

- To familiarize yourself with DOMC, try out this practice exam:

  https://sei.caveon.com/launchpad/docker-domc-practice-exam-world-geography/domc-practice

- DOMC answers are final. You cannot change them

- The best practice to train yourself for this type of questions is to study the wrong and the right choices in the sample questions listed in the next section and in Part 2.

Extra Resources

Google Forms for every exam section:

1. Orchestration: https://forms.gle/G4bfPQd91gJrDd39A

2. Networking: https://forms.gle/4KBK9d1Du89a1r347

3. Storage and volumes: https://forms.gle/CaMHDX1M63YD7Ypp7

4. Security: https://forms.gle/bvFwtu8hXvGvWEck8

5. Installation and configuration: https://forms.gle/Bd8HQ5fR9xCdFhuU9

6. Image creation, management, and registry: https://forms.gle/wiE5GWRCTTstUgUS7

The official study guide:

- https://training.mirantis.com/wp-content/uploads/2020/10/Docker-Study-Guide_v1.5-October.pdf

Links for the topics:

- https://github.com/DevOps-Academy-Org/dca-prep-guide

Questions per section:

- https://djitz.com/certification/docker-certified-associate-dca-certification-test-resources/

250 practice questions for the DCA Exam-Medium:

- `https://medium.com/bb-tutorials-and-thoughts/250-practice-questions-for-the-dca-exam-84f3b9e8f5ce`

DCA flashcards:

- `https://quizlet.com/at/416679132/docker-certified-associate-dca-prep-flash-cards/`

- `https://quizlet.com/de/324617753/dca-orchestration-flash-cards/`

Good luck! You can do it! ☺

PART II

Exam Prep Quizzes

CHAPTER 13

Orchestration Quiz

Note Always remember to check the questions listed in the "Extra Resources" section in Chapter 12.

---

1. In the context of a swarm-mode cluster, does this describe a node?

    A. A physical machine participating in the swarm

    B. An instance of the Docker engine participating in the swarm

    C. A virtual machine participating in the swarm

2. Two pods bear the same label, app: dev. Will a label selector matching app: dev match both pods?

    A. Yes, if all the containers in those pods are passing their livenessProbes and readinessProbes

    B. Yes, if both pods were preexisting when the label selector was declared

    C. Yes, if the pods are in the same Kubernetes namespace as the object bearing the label selector

    D. Yes, if the pods are in the same Kubernetes namespace as the object bearing the label selector and both pods were preexisting when the label selector was declared

3. Which of the following commands will create a swarm service that only listens on port 53 using UDP?

    A. docker service create --name dns-cache -p 53:53/udp dns-cache

© Engy Fouda 2022
E. Fouda, *A Complete Guide to Docker for Operations and Development*,
https://doi.org/10.1007/978-1-4842-8117-8_13

B. docker service create --name dns-cache -p 53:53 --service udp dns-cache

C. docker service create --name dns-cache -p 53:53 ..constraint networking.protocol.udp=true dns-cache

D. docker service create --name dns-cache -p 53:53 --udp dns-cache

4. After creating a new service named 'http', you notice that the new service is not registering as healthy. How do you view the list of historical tasks for that service by using the command line?

A. docker inspect http

B. docker service inspect http

C. docker service ps http

D. docker ps http

5. Which of the following modes can be used for service discovery of a Docker swarm service? (Choose two)

A. Virtual IP (VIP) with --endpoint-mode vip

B. Overlay with --endpoint-mode overlay

C. DNS Round-Robin with --endpoint-mode dnsrr

D. Ingress with --endpoint-mode ingress

E. Network Address Translation (NAT) with --endpoint-mode nat

6. You created a new service named 'http' and discover it is not registering as healthy. Will the command, docker service ps http, enable you to view the list of historical tasks for this service?

A. Yes

B. No

7. When seven managers are in a swarm cluster, how would they be distributed across three datacenters or availability zones?

    A. 5-1-1

    B. 3-2-2

    C. 3-3-1

    D. 4-2-1

8. A Docker service 'web' is running with a scale factor of 1 (replicas = 1). Bob intends to use the command 'docker service update --replicas=3 web'. Alice intends to use the command 'docker service scale web=3'. How do the outcomes of these two commands differ?

    A. Bob's command results in an error. Alice's command updates the number of replicas of the 'web' service to 3.

    B. Bob's command only updates the service definition, but no new replicas are started. Alice's command results in the actual scaling up of the 'web' service.

    C. Bob's command updates the number of replicas of the 'web' service to 3. Alice's command results in an error.

    D. Both Bob's and Alice's commands result in exactly the same outcome, which is 3 instances of the 'web' service.

9. You have just executed 'docker swarm leave' on a node. What command can be run on the same node to confirm it has left the cluster?

    A. docker node ls

    B. docker system info

    C. docker system status

    D. docker system status

10. What is the Docker command to set up a swarm?

    A. docker swarm init

    B. docker swarm create

    C. docker init swarm

    D. docker create swarm

11. What service mode is used to deploy a single task of a service to each node?

    A. Replicated

    B. Global

    C. Universal

    D. Distributed

Answer Key

1. B

2. D

3. A

4. B

5. A and C

6. B

7. B

8. D

9. B

10. A

11. B

CHAPTER 14

Image Creation, Management, and Registry Quiz

Note　Always remember to check the questions listed in the "Extra Resources" section in Chapter 12.

---

1. The following health check exists in a Dockerfile: `HEALTHCHECK CMD curl --fail http://localhost/health || exit 1`. Which of the following describes its purpose?

   A. Defines the action taken when container health fails, which in this case will kill the container with exit status 1

   B. Defines the health check endpoint on the localhost interface for external monitoring tools to monitor the health of the Docker engine

   C. Defines the health check endpoint on the localhost interface for containers to monitor the health of the Docker engine

   D. Defines the health check for the containerized application so that the application health can be monitored by the Docker engine

2. The output of which command can be used to find the architecture and operating system an image is compatible with.

© Engy Fouda 2022
E. Fouda, *A Complete Guide to Docker for Operations and Development*,
https://doi.org/10.1007/978-1-4842-8117-8_14

    A.   docker image inspect --filter {{.Architecture}} {{.OS}} '
           <image-id>

    B.   docker image ls <image-id>

    C.   docker image inspect –format='{{.Architecture}} {{.Os}} '
           <image-id>

    D.   docker image info <image-id>

3.   What is the purpose of multistage builds?

    A.   Better logical separation of Dockerfile instructions for better readability

    B.   Optimizing images by copying artifacts selectively from previous stages

    C.   Better caching when building Docker images

    D.   Faster image builds by allowing parallel execution of Docker builds

4.   From a DevOps process standpoint, it is best practice to keep changes to an application in version control. Which of the following will allow changes to a Docker image to be stored in a version control system?

    A.   docker commit

    B.   docker save

    C.   A docker-compose.yml file

    D.   A Dockerfile

5.   Which statement is true?

    A.   CMD shell format sometimes uses this form ["param", param", "param"].

    B.   ENTRYPOINT cannot be used in conjunction with CMD.

    C.   CMD is executed during the build time.

    D.   ENTRYPOINT cannot be overridden in the "docker container run" command.

6. Which of the following commands starts a Redis container and configures it to always restart unless it is explicitly stopped or Docker is restarted?

   A. docker run -d --restart-policy unless-stopped redis

   B. docker run -d --restart omit-stopped redis

   C. docker run -d --restart unless-stopped redis

   D. docker run -d --failure omit-stopped redis

7. What is the difference between the ADD and COPY Dockerfile instructions? (Choose two)

   A. ADD supports compression format handling, while COPY does not.

   B. COPY supports regular expression handling, while ADD does not.

   C. COPY supports compression format handling, while ADD does not.

   D. ADD support remote URL handling, while COPY does not.

   E. ADD supports regular expression handling, while COPY does not.

8. Some Docker images take time to build through a Continuous Integration environment. You want to speed up builds and take advantage of build caching. Where should the most frequently changed part of a Docker image be placed in a Dockerfile?

   A. At the bottom of the Dockerfile

   B. After the FROM directive

   C. At the top of the Dockerfile

   D. In the ENTRYPOINT directive

Answer Key

1. A

2. C

3. B

4. A

5. A

6. C. Please find the –restart options at the reference: `https://docs.docker.com/engine/reference/run/#restart-policies---restart`

7. D & E

8. A. Please read more at this link: `www.docker.com/blog/speed-up-your-development-flow-with-these-dockerfile-best-practices/`

CHAPTER 15

Installation and Configuration Quiz

Note Always remember to check the questions listed in the "Extra Resources" section in Chapter 12.

---

1. What is the Docker command to find the current logging driver for a running container?

   A. docker stats

   B. docker info

   C. docker config

   D. docker inspect

2. When an application being managed by the UCP fails, you would like a summary of all requests made to the UCP API in the hours leading up to the failure. What must be configured correctly beforehand for this to be possible?

   A. UCP audit logs must be set to the metadata or request level.

   B. UCP logging levels must be set to the info or debug level.

   C. All engines in the cluster must have their log driver set to the metadata or request level.

   D. Set the logging level in the config object for the ucp-kube-api-server container to warning or higher.

© Engy Fouda 2022
E. Fouda, *A Complete Guide to Docker for Operations and Development*,
https://doi.org/10.1007/978-1-4842-8117-8_15

3. A host machine has four CPUs available and two running containers. The sysadmin would like to assign two CPUs to each container. Which of the following commands achieves this?

    A. Set the '--cpuset-cpu's flag to '1.3' on one container and '2.4' on the other container.

    B. Set the '--cpuset-cpus' flag to '.5' on both containers.

    C. Set the '--cpuset-cpus' flag of the 'dockerd' process to the value 'even-spread'.

    D. Set the '--cpu-quota' flag to '1.3' on one container and '2,4' on the other container.

4. A user is having problems running Docker. Which of the following will start Docker in debug mode?

    A. Set the debug key to true in the 'daemon.json' file.

    B. Start the 'dockerd' process manually with the '--logging' flag set to debug.

    C. Set the logging key to debug in the 'daemon.json' file.

    D. Start the 'dockerd' process manually with the '--raw-logs' flag set to debug

5. Will this action upgrade Docker CE to Docker EE?

    A. Manually download the 'docker-ee' package.

    B. Uninstall the 'docker-ce' package before installing the 'docker-ee' package.

    C. Run the docker upgrade subcommand.

6. Following the principle of least privilege, which of the following methods can be used to securely grant access to a specific user to communicate to a Docker engine? (Choose two.)

    A. Utilize the '--host 0.0.0.0:2375' option to the Docker daemon to listen on port 2375 over TCP on all interfaces.

    B. Utilize openssl to create TLS client and server certificates, configuring the Docker engine to use with mutual TLS over TCP.

    C. Utilize the '--host 127.0.0.1:2375' option to the Docker daemon to listen on port 2375 over TCP on localhost.

    D. Give the user root access to the server to allow them to run Docker commands as root.

    E. Add the user to the 'docker' group on the server or specify the group with the '--group' Docker daemon option.

7. What is the purpose of a client bundle in the Universal Control Plane?

    A. Authenticate a user using client certificates to the Universal Control Plane.

    B. Provide a new user instruction for how to log in to the Universal Control Plane.

    C. Provide a user with a Docker client binary compatible with the Universal Control Plane.

    D. Group multiple users in a team in the Universal Control Plane.

8. What is used by the kernel to isolate resources when running Docker containers?

    A. Namespaces

    B. Overlay networks

    C. Volumes

    D. Control groups (also known as cgroups)

9. Does this describe the role of control groups (cgroups) when used with a Docker container? Solution: Role-Based Access Control to clustered resources

    A. Yes

    B. No

10. What is one way of directly transferring a Docker image from one Docker host to another?

    A. 'docker push' the image to the IP address of the target host.

    B. 'docker commit' to save the image outside of the Docker filesystem. Then transfer the file over to the target host and 'docker start' to start the container again.

    C. There is no way of directly transferring Docker images between hosts. A Docker registry must be used as an intermediary.

    D. 'docker save' the image to save it as a TAR file and copy it over to the target host. Then use 'docker load' to un-TAR the image back as a Docker image.

11. Which of the following are types of namespaces used by Docker to provide isolation? (Choose two.)

    A. Host

    B. Network

    C. Process ID

    D. Authentication

    E. Storage

12. What is the recommended way to configure the daemon flags and environment variables for your Docker daemon in a platform-independent way?

    A. Set the configuration options using the ENV variable.

    B. Set the configuration options in '/etc/docker/daemon.json'.

    C. Set the configuration DOCKER_OPTS in '/etc/default/docker'.

    D. Use 'docker config' to set the configuration options.

13. How do you change the default logging driver for the Docker daemon in Linux?

   A. Set the value of log-driver to the name of the logging driver in the daemon.json in /etc/doc.

   B. Use the -log-driver flag when you run a container.

   C. At the command line, type docker log driver set <driver name>.

   D. Install a logging agent on the Linux host.

Answer Key

1. D

2. A

3. B

4. A

5. B

6. B and E

7. A

8. D

9. B

10. D

11. B and C

12. B

13. D

CHAPTER 16

Networking Quiz

Note Always remember to check the questions listed in the "Extra Resources" section in Chapter 12.

---

1. The following Kubernetes YAML describes a ClusterIP service, where the service traffic is routed from which port to which one in a random pod with the label app: nginx?

```
apiversion:  v1
kind: Service
metadata:
  name: app
spec:
  type: clusterIP
  selector:
    app: nginx
  ports:
  - port: 8080
    targetport: 80
  - port: 5000
    targetport: 81
```

   A. From 8080 to 80

   B. From 8080 to 81

   C. From 8080 to 5000

   D. From 80 to 8080

© Engy Fouda 2022
E. Fouda, *A Complete Guide to Docker for Operations and Development,*
https://doi.org/10.1007/978-1-4842-8117-8_16

2. Which of the following is true about using the "-P" option when creating a new container?

    A. Docker binds each exposed container port to a random port on the host's interface.

    B. Docker gives extended privileges to the container.

    C. Docker binds each exposed container port to a random port on a specified host interface.

    D. Docker binds each exposed container port with the same port on the host.

3. Which of the following is true about overlay networks?

    A. Overlay networks are created only on the manager node that you created the overlay networking on.

    B. Overlay networks are created on all cluster nodes when you create the overlay network.

    C. Overlay networks are first created on the manager nodes. Then they are created on the worker nodes once a task is scheduled on the specific worker node.

    D. Overlay networks are only created on the manager nodes.

4. True or false: To make containers – connected on a bridge network – accessible outside the host, you use either EXPOSE or --publish to access the containers on the bridge network.

    A. True

    B. False

5. The following Kubernetes YAML will block which traffic?

    ```
    apiversion: networking.k8s.io/v1
    kind: NetworkPolicy
    metadata:
      name: app
      namespace: app
    ```

```
spec:
  podSelector:
    matchLabels:
      tier:  frontend
  ingress:
  -from:
    -podSelector:
      matchLabels:
        tier:  backend
```

A. A request issued from a pod lacking the tier: backend label to a pod bearing the tier:frontend label

B. A request issued from a pod lacking the tier: frontend label to a pod bearing the tier:backend label

C. A request issued from a pod lacking the tier: backend label to a pod bearing the tier:backend label

D. A request issued from a pod lacking the tier: frontend label to a pod bearing the tier:frontend label

6. True or false: To make containers – connected on a bridge network – accessible outside the host, you use `network connect` to access the containers on the bridge network.

   A. True

   B. False

7. How to create a container that is reachable from its host network?

   A. Use `network attach` to access the container on the bridge network.

   B. Use `--link` to access the container on the bridge network.

   C. Use either `EXPOSE` or `--publish` to access the container on the bridge network.

8. Which networking drivers allow you to enable multi-host network connectivity between containers?

    A. macvlan, ipvlan, and overlay

    B. bridge, user-defined, host

    C. bridge, macvlan, ipvlan, overlay

    D. host, macvlan, overlay, user-defined

9. How to ensure that overlay traffic between service tasks is encrypted?

    A. docker network create -d overlay -o encrypted=true <network-name>

    B. In the docker-compose file, in the networks section, add encrypted: 'yes', as in the following code:

        ```
        networks:
          frontend:
          backend:
          payment:
            driver:  overlay
            encrypted:  'yes'
        ```

    C. docker network create -d overlay –secure

    D. docker service create --network <network-name> --encrypted <service-name>

    E. Answers A and B

10. How to obtain the published port(s) of a container?

    A. docker container inspect

    B. docker port

    C. docker container ls

    D. All the above

Answer Key

1. A

2. A

3. B

4. A

5. A

6. B

7. C

8. A

9. E

10. D

CHAPTER 17

Security Quiz

Note Always remember to check the questions listed in the "Extra Resources" section in Chapter 12.

---

1. What is the purpose of DCT?

   A. Sign and verify image tags.

   B. It is correlated with TLS.

   C. Sign images pushed and pulled to and from the registry.

   D. A and C

2. You export the environment variable DOCKER_CONTENT_TRUST=1. If you try to pull example/image:latest, which is an unsigned image, what will happen?

   A. Docker blocks this command.

   B. docker service creates example/image:latest

   C. Docker will generate an error.

   D. A and C

3. To push a verified image to a registry, what environment variable do you export to sign the image?

   A. DOCKER_IMAGE_SIGN=1

   B. NOTARY_ENABLE=1

   C. DOCKER_CONTENT_TRUST=0

   D. DOCKER_CONTENT_TRUST=1

© Engy Fouda 2022
E. Fouda, *A Complete Guide to Docker for Operations and Development*,
https://doi.org/10.1007/978-1-4842-8117-8_17

4. Which of these are false about secrets?

   A. Use standard input (STDIN) and a file to create secrets.

   B. You can create and manage secrets with the `docker secret` sub-command.

   C. You can attach them to services by specifying the `--secret` flag to the docker service create command.

   D. All of the above

   E. None of the above

Answer Key

1. D

2. A

3. D

4. E

CHAPTER 18

Storage and Volumes Quiz

Note Always remember to check the questions listed in the "Extra Resources" section in Chapter 12.

---

1. Which of these commands will display a list of volumes for a specific container?

    A. docker volume logs nginx --containers

    B. docker volume inspect nginx

    C. docker container logs nginx –volumes

    D. docker container inspect nginx

2. A container named "test" that stores results in a volume called "vol" was created by running this command: `docker run -d –name test -v vol:/vol vote`. How are the results accessed in "vol" with another container called "test2"?

    A. docker run -d --name test2 --volume test vote

    B. docker run -d --name test2 --mount test vote

    C. docker run -d –name test2 --volume vol vote

    D. docker run -d --name test2 --volumes-from test vote

3. You want to mount external storage to a particular filesystem path in a container in a Kubernetes pod. What is the correct set of objects to use for this?

© Engy Fouda 2022
E. Fouda, *A Complete Guide to Docker for Operations and Development*,
https://doi.org/10.1007/978-1-4842-8117-8_18

    A. A storageClass in the pod's specification, populated with a volume that is bound to a provisioner defined by a persistentVolume

    B. A volume in the pod's specification, populated with a storageClass that is bound to a provisioner defined by a persistentVolume

    C. A persistentVolume in the pod's specification, populated with a persistentVolumeClaim that is bound to a volume defined by a storageClass

4. How to mount a read-only volume?

    A. docker run -d --name=nginxtest --mount source=nginx-vol,destination=/usr/share/nginx/html,readonly nginx:latest

    B. docker run -d --name=nginxtest -v nginx-vol:/usr/share/nginx/html:ro nginx:latest

    C. All of the above

5. Which devicemapper mode should be configured for production?

    A. direct-lvm

    B. loop-lvm

    C. overlay-lvm

    D. aufs-lvm

6. Which devicemapper mode uses loopback and is used for rudimentary testing prior to production?

    A. direct-lvm

    B. loop-lvm

    C. overlay-lvm

    D. aufs-lvm

7. Which one of the following commands will result in the volume being removed automatically once the container has exited?

    A. docker container run --del -v /vol ubuntu

    B. docker container run --rm -v ubuntu

    C. docker container run --rm -v /vol ubuntu

    D. docker container run --remove -v /vol Ubuntu

    E. B and C

8. Which of the following constitutes a production-ready devicemapper configuration for the Docker engine?

    A. Create a volume group in devicemapper and utilize the '--dm.thinpooldev' Docker daemon option, specifying the volume group.

    B. Format a partition with xfs and mount it at '/var/lib/docker'.

    C. Utilize the '--storage-opt dm.directlvm_device' Docker daemon option, specifying a block device.

    D. Nothing. Devicemapper comes ready for production usage out of the box.

9. A persistentVolumeClaim (PVC) is created with the specification storageClass: " " and size requirements that cannot be satisfied by any existing persistentVolume. How will Kubernetes act?

    A. The PVC remains unbound until a persistentVolume that matches all requirements of the PVC becomes available.

    B. Kubernetes will combine several PVs to fulfill the PVC requirement.

    C. Kubernetes will reconfigure the SC.

    D. The PVC will get bound to the available PV even if its size is smaller.

10.   Which one of the following commands will show a list of volumes for a specific container?

A.   docker container logs <container name> --volumes

B.   docker container inspect <container name>

C.   docker volume inspect <container name>

D.   docker volume logs <container name> --containers

Answer Key

1.   D

2.   D

3.   A

4.   C

5.   A

6.   B

7.   E

8.   C

9.   A

10.   B

Index

© Engy Fouda 2022
E. Fouda, *A Complete Guide to Docker for Operations and Development*,
https://doi.org/10.1007/978-1-4842-8117-8